© 1992 Trustees of
the British Museum
Published by
British Museum Press
A division of British
Museum Publications Ltd
46 Bloomsbury Street,
London WC1B 3QQ

British Library Cataloguing
in Publication Data
Eames, Elizabeth
  Tilers. — (Medieval
  craftsmen)
  I. Title II. Series
  738.6
ISBN 0-7141-2053-7

Designed by Roger Davies
Set in Palatino by Southern
Positives and Negatives
(SPAN), Lingfield, Surrey
Printed and bound in
Singapore

Front cover Painting from an
illuminated manuscript
showing St Edmund standing
on a pavement of glazed tiles
to receive King Offa's ring.

Back cover Part of a panel from
Rievaulx Abbey. See Fig. 33.

Title page Manuscript
illustration of a mid-fifteenth-
century Flemish brickworks.
The kiln is a far more
sophisticated structure than
any known medieval English
tile kiln but the forming shed,
hacksteads and the activities
portrayed are what one would
expect to see in a medieval
English tilery.

*This page Brickmakers near
Hemiksen*, by David Teniers the
Younger (1610–90) showing a
Dutch brickworks.

Contents

Known kiln sites and other probable centres of production of decorated medieval tiles.

KEY

Chertsey	Excavated tile kiln
Ashstead	Excavated kiln with some associated tiles
Bagley Wood	Kiln suggested by wasters
Barnstaple	Documentary or other evidence for kiln

North Berwick ●
● Newbattle Abbey

● Rievaulx Abbey
●Byland Abbey

● York

North Grange Meaux ●

● Norton Priory
● Denbigh ●Chester
Toynton ●
Nottingham ● ● Haverholme Priory
Hulton Abbey ● ● Dale Abbey ● ●Lenton Priory
● Repton Priory
● Burton Lazars
● Bawsey
Lilleshall Abbey ● ● Great Saredon
● Polesworth
● Wenlock Priory ● Chilvers Coton
Halesowen Abbey ● Stoke Pipewell ● Lyvedon Ramsey Abbey
Coventry Abbey ● Ely
● Droitwich ● Diddington
● Great Malvern
● Hanley Castle Chetwode Priory
● Hailes Abbey ● Little Brickhill
Cadmer End, Thame ● Stebbing
Bagley Wood ● Mill Green Ingatestone ● Pleshey Castle
● Penn ● Danbury
Farringdon Street London ●
Clowes Wood
● Bristol Canterbury
Keynsham Abbey ● ● Nash Hill ● Newbury ● Chertsey Boxley
Lacock Great Bedwin Abbey
Tyler Hill, Canterbury
● Barnstaple ● Newark Priory Ashstead
● Shulbrede
● Taunton Clarendon ● Rye
Palace Otterbourne Battle ●
● Binstead
● Fordington

INTRODUCTION

The first tilers to work in Britain were Roman military craftsmen who came over with Claudius' army in AD 43. Extensive workshops belonging to the legion stationed in Chester have been found and excavated at Holt on the River Dee. These included a bank of four large tile kilns and several pottery kilns. Numerous Roman tile kilns have been found in the south of England and the products of some of these were stamped with the initials of the British fleet, demonstrating that these also were the work of legionary tilers. It is quite possible that there were civilian tilers who had learnt their craft under the legionary craftsmen but there is at present no proof of this. There will have been no military tilers in Britain after AD 410, when the last imperial forces were withdrawn, and it would seem that even if there were some civilian tilers their craft quickly died out.

The Roman tilers made three types of tile: roof tiles which form the bulk of their production, building tiles or bricks, and square tiles for floors. In Britain their building tiles were about 30 cm (1 ft) square and 2.5–3 cm (1–1$\frac{1}{2}$ in) thick. On the Continent many walls were built entirely of such tiles but in England they seem generally to have been used for bonding and levelling courses in walls constructed of flint or stone rubble.

The pagan Anglo-Saxons, who quickly overran the lowland zone of England in the first half of the fifth century AD, built in wood and had no use for stone or tiles. It was not until after the mission of St Augustine to Kent in AD 597 that masonwork was again introduced in the building of churches. We know from the Venerable Bede that masons were imported from the Continent to build the earliest churches, and excavations have revealed that three of these, St Pancras, SS. Peter and Paul and St Mary, all on the site of the later St Augustine's Abbey in Canterbury, were built of reused Roman building tiles.

Roman roofs were made with two different shapes of tile: a large, flat tegula with flanged

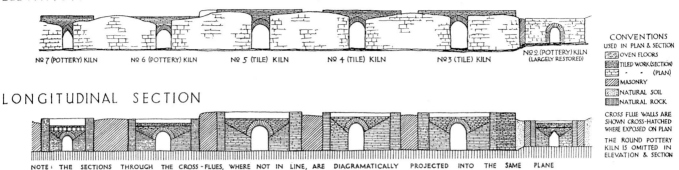

ELEVATION

Nº 7 (POTTERY) KILN   Nº 6 (POTTERY) KILN   Nº 5 (TILE) KILN   Nº 4 (TILE) KILN   Nº 3 (TILE) KILN   Nº 2 (POTTERY) KILN (LARGELY RESTORED)

LONGITUDINAL SECTION

NOTE: THE SECTIONS THROUGH THE CROSS-FLUES, WHERE NOT IN LINE, ARE DIAGRAMATICALLY PROJECTED INTO THE SAME PLANE

CONVENTIONS
USED IN PLAN & SECTION
OVEN FLOORS
TILED WORK (SECTION)
" " (PLAN)
MASONRY
NATURAL SOIL
NATURAL ROCK

CROSS FLUE WALLS ARE
SHOWN CROSS-HATCHED
WHERE EXPOSED ON PLAN

THE ROUND POTTERY
KILN IS OMITTED IN
ELEVATION & SECTION

GENERAL PLAN

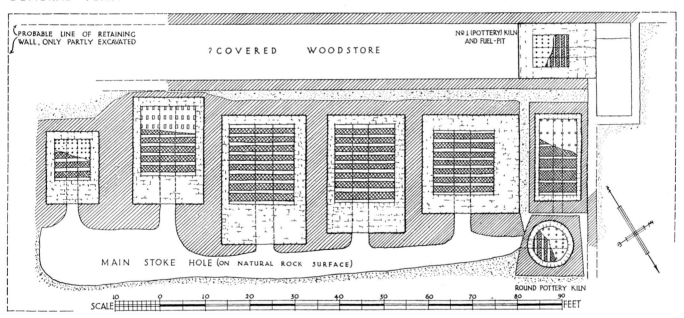

PROBABLE LINE OF RETAINING WALL, ONLY PARTLY EXCAVATED

? COVERED WOODSTORE

Nº 1 (POTTERY) KILN AND FUEL-PIT

MAIN STOKE HOLE (ON NATURAL ROCK SURFACE)

ROUND POTTERY KILN

SCALE   10   0   10   20   30   40   50   60   70   80   90   FEET

1 *Opposite* Places in Britain where medieval tilers are known to have been producing decorated floor tiles.

2 Plan, elevation and section of the bank of tile and pottery kilns on the site of the Roman legionary workshops at Holt, Denbigh. Excavated *c.*1911.

sides and an imbrex, a truncated half-cone. The imbrices were set in vertical rows covering the flanges of the tegulae. There is no evidence that such tiles were later reused on roofs but plain, flat roofing tiles have been found during excavation on some late Anglo-Saxon sites. These bear no resemblance to any of the Roman forms and it seems probable that tilers had established an industry for manufacturing roof tiles in East

Anglia and possibly in Middlesex by the later tenth century. No tilery of this period has yet been located.

At the same time the first decorated floor tiles known in England were being made. Examples have been found at Winchester, Bury St Edmunds, St Albans, Polesworth and York, all monastic sites founded or refounded in the second half of the tenth century. The surface of

3 Medieval ridge and roof tiles of the thirteenth century. *Left* Pieces of glazed roof tile from the site of Clarendon Palace, Wiltshire. *Centre top* Crested ridge tile from Eresby Manor, Lincolnshire. *Centre bottom* Cut-out ridge crest from the kiln site at Haverholme Priory, Lincolnshire. *Right* Roof tiles and glazed crested ridge tile from the site of Clarendon Palace.

these tiles was divided into separate cells by raised half-round mouldings and each cell was glazed, usually with a different colour from its neighbours. No tilery associated with these tiles has yet been found. It is possible that the tilers were itinerant. The production of these tiles was short-lived and it was at least two hundred years before any lasting decorated floor-tile industry was established.

Although there is no firm evidence, we may suppose that once East Anglian tilers had begun to produce a fireproof and weatherproof ceramic roof tile, the manufacture of such tiles would have continued and spread to other parts of lowland England. Certainly by the twelfth century roof tiles were being widely manufactured and by the beginning of the thirteenth century some were furnished with an apron of lead glaze. This provided a more waterproof and colourful roof. Such tiles have been found on the roof of the Deanery at Winchester and during excavations on the site of Clarendon **3** Palace, where they were probably made. A twelfth-century kiln for the firing of such tiles was excavated on the site of Guildford Castle in 1991.

By the thirteenth century and possibly earlier, tilers were making ridge tiles. Many of these had elaborate crests and other decoration applied to **3** them and their upper parts were lead glazed. In Northamptonshire and other counties where stone tiles or slates formed the main roof, such glazed ceramic tiles were used for the ridge. The tilers who made decorated ridge tiles may also have made plain roof tiles. However, the excavated site of a tilery at Haverholme Priory in Lincolnshire, where the structures had been heavily destroyed by ploughing, produced kiln furniture and wasters of decorated and glazed ridge tiles but no plain roof tiles.

4 Fifteenth-century manuscript painting of William Bruges, first Garter King of Arms. He is shown kneeling before St George and the dragon on a pavement of plain glazed tiles. Such arrangements of tiles glazed in different colours, often imported from the Netherlands, were popular in the fifteenth and sixteenth centuries.

The manufacture of decorated and plain glazed floor tiles was probably fully developed on the Continent before it was introduced to England and it is therefore probable that the first English examples were made by foreign tilers. Some may have been pressed into the service of the king, while others may have moved to England with their monastic order.

At first the tilers making decorated floor tiles worked on special commissions manufacturing them as near as possible to the place where they were to be used. A useful body of information about the tilers who worked for the king is preserved in the surviving accounts of royal building works. In the thirteenth century the king's tilers were paid a daily wage and doubtless also had rations of bread and beer, but by the fourteenth century they were being paid per thousand tiles either manufactured or laid. There is more documentary information about roof tiles than floor tiles because there was a greater demand for them. The interpretation of the records, however, is complicated by the fact that the same word is used for the man who made roof tiles, the man who made floor tiles and the man who hung them on the roof or laid them on the floor.

Some large religious houses could call upon the labour of their lay brothers to make elaborate tile mosaics. In the Cistercian houses a number of the monks themselves probably took part, not only in the organisation of the work, but also in the actual making of the tiles, thus fulfilling their vows to serve God partly through manual labour.

It seems likely that, although for the first decades after their introduction decorated tiles could be afforded only by the king and the greater religious houses, there was a gradual increase in demand from rich magnates and wealthy merchants. They did not have the space to set up a tilery on their own premises just for their particular project, so commercial tileries came into production, making tiles for many customers who paid separately for their transport by road or water. It seems that sometimes a tilery that had been set up for a specific commission continued to operate commercially after the original order had been fulfilled. Although it was thought that commercial tileries were not established before the fourteenth century, it is now known that several were operating during the later thirteenth century, one possibly before 1260. Even after the introduction of commercial products, it was still possible for a patron who could afford it to have elaborate and expensive pavements specially made. The Black Death seems to have put an end to that for several decades during which almost no one could afford commissioned tiles, instead they had to buy mass-produced tiles from an established tilery. This was because many craftsmen will have died in the pestilence and those who survived could demand higher wages and charge more for their products. The wealthy on the other hand, suffered severe losses of rents and trade and were comparatively impoverished: even the King's Clerks of Works were content to use the good commercial products.

Archaeological evidence from a number of excavated kiln sites which have yielded more roof tiles than decorated floor tiles suggests that the maker of decorated floor tiles would sometimes join a tilery making roof tiles rather than set up in an entirely new location. There would be many advantages in this: the occupant of the tilery making roof tiles would own or lease clay pits and have access to a good supply of fuel; he would have an organised system of distribution for his products. The maker of decorated floor tiles might stay in one tilery all his working life or he might stay there for a time and then move on when demand in the area was satisfied.

The men who made decorated floor tiles were specialists, whether they were working on particular orders or for a general market. They possessed a store of knowledge about the methods of decoration, the combination of different clays, the making of glazes and the construction of kilns that would reach the required temperature, far beyond the knowledge necessary for the tiler who made roof tiles, even if he sometimes produced glazed wares. Nevertheless, it is probable that many roof-tile makers tried their hands at making decorated floor tiles. Only so can one account for the many local oddities, well out of the general trend, that are present up and down the country, some of them perhaps made to carry out repairs.

We do not know the names of any of the designers who drew the decorative patterns. They probably ranged from such artists as Henry III's painters, Master William and Master Walter of Durham, to the son of the local tiler whittling out a pattern on a block of wood in the winter evenings. One suspects that every now and again, when special tiles were commissioned, a competent artist drew the designs and a competent carver cut the stamps with which the decoration was applied. The artist and carver may often have been the same person, but whether he was also a tile maker is more doubtful. Once these stamps were made, they were reused until they wore out. They were

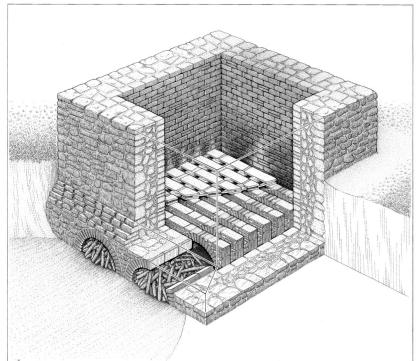

5 Reconstruction of a roof tile kiln, dating to the second quarter of the thirteenth century, found during excavation in Borelli Yard, Farnham, Surrey, in 1985–6.

copied many times, often until the original design was scarcely recognisable. Besides copying stamps, the carver might also make more fashionable variations on the same themes: the elaboration of the fleur-de-lis as a motif demonstrates this.

It is probable that at all times, except between about 1350 and 1380, tilers could be found who would execute special orders for an enhanced price. When new designs were made for such special jobs, they then passed into the common repertory, which was thus replenished: there was no copyright on a design, even when it included personal names and heraldry.

Medieval tilers could earn their living in a number of different ways. The makers of roof tiles were probably usually dependent upon selling their products in the open market. Those who made the decorated ridge tiles at Haverholme Priory worked in the precinct and may have been lay brothers because Haverholme was originally a Cistercian house and some of their kiln furniture resembles that found at North Grange, Meaux, another Cistercian house, where we know that the tilery was run by lay brothers. However, comparable ridge tiles have been found elsewhere in Lincolnshire, which suggests that the Haverholme tiles may have been sold commercially. At Clarendon Palace it may be supposed that the tilers who made the glazed roof and ridge tiles set up their tilery within the precinct. The site of this tilery has not been found but its products were available to the tiler who set up his kiln there about 1240 to make the tiles for the king's new chapel. He was employed by Elias of Dyrham, the King's Clerk in charge of the work at Clarendon. He and his mates will all have been paid a day wage, at that time probably about eight pence for the master and less for his assistants; the decorated floor-tile maker may have been paid a little more. It is clear that if the King's Clerk of Works wanted the service of a particular tiler he could demand his presence at once, wherever he happened to be working; it seems certain that the tiler making the decorated tiles for the king's chapel at Clarendon Palace had already been working at Beaulieu Abbey and St Denys' Priory in Southampton.

The records of Battle Abbey reveal that some tilers leased their kilns from wealthy owners while others may have had their own. In 1373 one Peter at Gate leased land at Wye in Kent, on which tileries were situated. He obtained this at a low rent on condition that he 'served as the Lord's workman for making tiles'.

Tilers fulfilling a special order were paid either a day wage or a fixed sum for the job. Those who worked commercially, selling their tiles on the open market, had to adjust their costs and prices to ensure that they made a profit. They usually made their tiles smaller and used less white clay in order to reduce the quantity of their raw materials. It has been estimated that the amount of clay used to make one Great Malvern tile would made $1\frac{1}{2}$ thirteenth-century Wessex tiles, $2\frac{1}{2}$ Penn tiles or $3\frac{1}{2}$ Bawsey tiles. An oven that would hold 1,000 Great Malvern tiles would hold 1,500 Wessex tiles, 2,500 Penn tiles and 3,500 Bawsey tiles. These are rough figures but they demonstrate that the successful commercial tilers could make a far greater number of tiles from the same amount of clay and using the same amount of fuel, for only one loading and unloading of the oven. It was not only the commercial tilers who gradually reduced the amount of the more expensive white clay that they had to import. The method of pouring a thin slip used very successfully by the Great Malvern and Bristol tilers was highly economical of white clay. Not all tilers imported china clay from Cornwall: Winchester College paid for white clay from Farnham, Surrey, and its transport to the tilery at Otterbourne. There were probably other small pockets of white-firing clay that local tilers could exploit scattered about the country.

After the middle of the fourteenth century few if any tilers making decorated floor tiles scooped keys or stabbed the backs of their tiles, whether they were making for a special order or commercially. This eliminated one process from the manufacture, thus saving time.

The quality of decoration of commercial tiles began to deteriorate towards the end of the fourteenth century and the decoration of two-colour tiles known to date from the earlier fifteenth century is very poor indeed. The revival of quality came with the mid-fifteenth-century tilers at Great Malvern Priory, who set up their tilery on the site in the old way and decorated their tiles with specially prepared designs. For the next hundred years wealthy patrons were commissioning pavements specially designed for them. Commercial production continued, and in some cases the quality of decoration was apparently unaffected by this revival as can be seen, for example, in the products of the Little Brickhill tilery.

The London tilers were never permitted to form a Guild. No doubt they were despised by the City Fathers, dominated by the Goldsmiths, Mercers, Vintners and Grocers with their precious metal, imported silks, wines and spices. Perhaps they were regarded as little better than the charcoal burners, living in the woods, providing London with smokeless fuel. Certainly the tilers' work was dirty, their wet clay stuck to everything and their kilns belched forth smoke and noisome fumes. They were

probably forbidden to work within the confines of the city itself, but they managed to set up very close by. One of their kilns was discovered at Farringdon Street when the Metropolitan railway, the earliest part of the London Underground was under construction. There is documentary evidence that tilers were working in Westminster in the thirteenth century. In Coventry they were more highly respected and were allowed to form a Guild, but again the only kiln associated with their industry found so far was located outside the city in the suburban area at Stoke.

Whatever their social standing, even the humblest tilers were producing fireproof roof-covering and ventilators at a price that people could afford in areas where stone tiles were not available. The very rich could use lead, but even royal buildings were often roofed with wooden shingles and the commonest roofing material was thatch. When one remembers that most medieval buildings had an open hearth in the middle of the main living room, a roof covering of combustible material was a serious fire hazard.

London suffered many disastrous fires before the famous fire of 1666. After one of the medieval fires the City Fathers decreed that all houses were to be roofed with tiles. What a boost for the London roof-tile industry! Unfortunately, like many a boom, it brought trouble in its wake. Tilers found themselves in court and fined for selling as first-class material the underfired tiles from the outside of their stacks. These proved to be porous and tended to crumble. One can imagine the pressures of this sudden demand. The number of skilled men may have been increased by recruiting from nearby industries, but even so, the task would have taken some time. The important members of the community will doubtless have harassed the tilers to give them immediate priority and the poor will have huddled under a temporary covering until their turn to have the necessary tiles came round at last. Few glazed roof tiles and fancy decorated ridges can have been made in London at this time. Even when the tiles had been supplied the purchaser had to wait for a skilled craftsman to hang them on the roof.

6, 71, 72, 73

6 The tilers who made these heraldic wall tiles, specially designed for Great Malvern Priory, set up their workshops and kilns in the precinct east of the church in the 1450s. The illustration shows tiles in the reredos south of the High Altar.

Work in medieval tileries was seasonal. The materials tilers needed for ridge tiles and glazed roof tiles were identical, but in addition they needed white-firing clay for some of their floor tiles. The basic raw material was clay, which was readily available in most areas of lowland England. The tilers dug this in the autumn and carted it to their yards where it was left in heaps until Christmas, then turned over at least once and left until the spring. During the winter the frost and rain broke up the clods and washed out some of the foreign matter. Very little further preparation was undertaken, although sand was sometimes added as a filler.

In the spring some of this clay and any waste tiles that were still lying about were used to carry out any necessary repairs to the kiln, and in the building of new kilns. The fired tiles of which the kilns were constructed were bonded together with clay which turned into a ceramic when the kilns were fired. Mortar could not be used for this purpose.

There are no known contemporary representations of an English tilery but medieval Netherlandish illustrations of the building of the Tower of Babel often show a brickworks. A mid-fifteenth-century Netherlandish manuscript of Bible History, now in the British Library, shows such a brickworks which, apart from the sophisticated kiln, might well be a medieval English tilery. The tilers probably began to form their tiles in April or May in an open-fronted shed containing long forming tables. The site of one such shed was found at the thirteenth- to fourteenth-century tilery excavated at Danbury in Essex, where both plain glazed and decorated floor tiles were made as well as roof tiles. Clay was taken into the shed and stones and other visible pieces of foreign matter were removed by hand. The roof-tile makers may have rolled out a slab of clay on the sanded forming table and cut the edges round templates, or they may have used a shallow wooden form in which to shape the tiles. The form was a wooden box

without top or bottom that was placed on the forming table and the clay pressed into it. Whichever method was used, the tilers levelled the top of their tiles by cutting off the surplus clay with a bow that probably had a wire string. They then smoothed the surface with a wet wooden strike which also broke down the clay into smaller particles leaving the top finer. The appearance of these medieval roof tiles suggests that after the tilers had scraped the surface they removed the form and then pressed the long sides of the tiles lightly together between two wooden bats which left a low, irregular ridge at each long side of the tile slightly above the level of the surface. This would guide rainwater running down the tiles away from the joins between them.

The medieval roof-tile makers had two ways of preparing the tiles to be hung over the battens of the roof. Their commonest method was to stab two holes about 1 cm in diameter and 1 cm below the top of the tile and equidistant from both sides. The tiler who hung the tiles inserted wooden pegs through these holes and hung them over the battens. Less frequently, the tiler took an extra piece of clay, fixed it onto the back of the tile at the top and shaped it into a nib which was then hung over the batten. Some tiles have been found where the tiler had made both a nib and one peg hole. The roof tiles were hung so that the upper two-thirds of one row was covered by the row above. The tiler who glazed his roof tiles glazed only the bottom third of the surface. No tiler treated the backs, and the marks of the sand on which the roof tiles were formed are always apparent.

The tilers who made ridge tiles cut out larger slabs from their rolled-out clay, scraped the surface and batted up the sides. They then bent the tiles over so that the top was curved and the two sides were at an angle of about forty-five degrees. Some tilers merely glazed the top of their ridges but most applied some other form of decoration first. Crests, some of them very

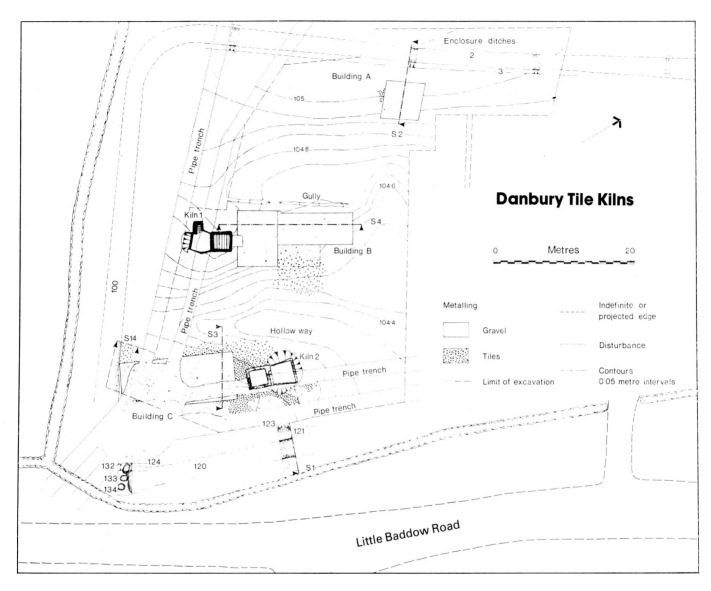

Danbury Tile Kilns

Enclosure ditches

Building A

Pipe trench

Gully

Kiln 1

Building B

Pipe trench

S14

S3

Hollow way

Kiln 2

Building C

Pipe trench

Pipe trench

Little Baddow Road

0   Metres   20

Metalling

Gravel

Tiles

Limit of excavation

Indefinite or projected edge

Disturbance

Contours 0·05 metre intervals

7 Plan of a commercial tilery at Danbury, near Chelmsford, Essex, showing the sites of two kilns, three workshops, a house and ancillary structures. Excavated in 1974.

elaborate, were the most popular. The tiler made these by wiping an extra strip of clay along the top of the ridge tile and cutting it into decorative shapes. Sometimes he applied straps of twisted or stamped clay to the main part of the ridge tile, or he stamped decoration directly on to the tile itself. Such decoration can scarcely have been visible from the ground. The crests, which were generally glazed, were by far the most effective ornament.

Before the end of the twelfth century some tilers were making plain and decorated glazed floor tiles. The tiler producing floor tiles also made them in a form on a sanded table. He may have been a little more careful to remove foreign material from the clay, but many tiles have been found where a stone was included in the body and when the clay shrank during drying and firing the stone split the surface and spoilt the tile. After he had pressed the clay into his form, the tiler also cut off the surplus with a bow and smoothed the surface with a strike, as described above.

All tiles, when they had been formed were removed to a drying place or 'hackstead'. This was often out of doors and indeed, some tiles show the footprints of small animals or birds that had walked over them. Some more important floor tiles were dried in a shed. One of the structures discovered at Danbury had a hearth in it and is thought to have been used as a drying shed. This was probably unusual. Even in the twentieth century some tileries still used unheated but well-ventilated drying sheds with slatted sides that can be opened or closed according to the weather. Medieval drying sheds may have had shutters to be used in the same way, but even so drying would be hindered by persistent wet weather. When the tiles were leather-hard they were returned to the board or forming table, decorated, trimmed round the edges, and glazed. They were then ready to fire.

THE GLAZES
Medieval tilers needed lead for all their glazes. One manuscript describes how to make a frit by making glass in a small furnace, pouring it out onto the ground to cool and pulverising the glass sheet. This powdered glass was to be mixed with the lees of wine or small beer and brushed onto the dried but unfired tiles. This method may sometimes have been used, but there is both documentary and archaeological evidence for a simpler way of making the glaze. The tilers put lead, probably scrap, into an iron pan and placed it in a furnace where they raked it with an iron rake until it had turned into an ash of lead oxide. They brushed this on to the surface of the dried tiles and left it to combine with the silica and alumina in the clay during firing. The glaze so formed made a close bond with the fabric of the tiles. Although it was slightly less glossy than the pre-prepared glazes which later tilers applied to pre-fired tiles, it was harder wearing and did not crackle or flake off. It is possible that they sometimes used powdered galena, lead sulphide, instead of lead oxide, but there is no proof of this. Traces of ash of lead oxide were found in the excavation of two small ovens at the Danbury tilery, and also in the remains of a large flat pottery dish excavated on the site of the tile kilns at North Grange, Meaux.

All these lead glazes were contaminated with iron, partly because of the iron pan and rake with which the ash was prepared and partly because the clay bodies with which they combined usually contained iron. The result of this was that the glaze looked yellow over white clay or slip and brown over a red body. If the body was reduced and grey in colour the glaze looked a dull olive green. In a pavement laid in the new eastern arm of the abbey church at Hailes, Gloucestershire, completed in 1278, the tilers made use of the different colour of the oxidised and reduced tiles. Each panel in the pavement was laid with tiles of one design but reduced and oxidised examples were generally laid alternately to produce a chequered result. The tilers there were clearly capable of controlling the oxygen in their kilns during the last stage of firing to produce either oxidised or reduced wares.

Most tilers, however, did not rely on body colour to provide different coloured tiles but added other metals to their basic lead glaze. Commonest of these was copper or brass to

8 Tilers' tools used in the nineteenth or early twentieth century, probably only a little different from those used by medieval tilers. *Top* A bow and a form; *bottom* a draw-knife and a strike.

9 A tiler's form and a template for a ridge tile crest made and used in 1990 by Michael Page to form replicas of nineteenth-century copies of medieval examples.

produce green. There is documentary evidence for this, in which the tilers are told to introduce copper or brass as filings. It is clear that these were merely mixed with the dry lead ash. As a result, green did not mix evenly in the glaze when it fluxed but remained in dark specks or streaks in a lighter green glaze. However accidental, this effect is often very pleasing. When they wanted a black or near-black glaze the tilers merely added a higher percentage of copper or brass. Tiles with this glaze were very frequently used as borders outlining panels in the floor. There is little evidence that manganese was used in England. Iron was occasionally added to produce a near-black brown. There is no apparent difference in the appearance of these near-black glazes, whether used over a red oxidised or grey reduced body.

Such dark-glazed, undecorated tiles were often used with undecorated light-glazed examples. In order to achieve a light colour the tilers had to coat the surface of the tile with a white-firing slip, over which the glaze looked yellow. A white slip was also used for the decoration of two-colour tiles. There are few places in England where a truly white-firing clay is available and such examples as have been analysed have proved to contain kaolinite. This is present in Cornwall and must have been imported by the tilers who used it. There is no doubt that it was expensive. There is, however, documentary evidence that the white-firing clay that outcrops in Farnham Park and Cheam Park and was the basis of the Surrey whiteware pottery industry was purchased from Farnham by tilers in Hampshire. It is likely that other tilers in the area also used this, and there may well have been local sources in other parts of the country.

THE KILNS

While early medieval pottery kilns were still simple structures that were little more than clay-lined holes in the ground for the furnaces with temporary ovens, the kilns built by roof-tile makers were already more sophisticated. These consisted of a rectangular furnace below ground to provide support and insulation. This had two or three parallel furnace chambers, each fired from a fire-box at the downhill stoke-hole end. The furnace chambers were arched over to support the floor of a rectangular, straight-sided oven. This had no permanent roof and after it had been loaded it was closed by a temporary roof of three or more layers of already fired tile bonded together with clay. The tilers did not construct a doorway or 'gate' in the walls of their ovens, which meant that they had to climb over the wall to load and unload the tiles. No oven is known to survive to its full height but the oven of kiln 1 at Danbury survived to a height of 84 cm (2 ft 9 in). One may suppose about 120 cm (4 ft) to be the maximum height over which the tilers could climb easily to load and unload their ovens.

At the rear of a later thirteenth-century roof-tile kiln excavated at North Grange, Meaux Abbey in Yorkshire, where the furnace area was above ground because of the wetness of the site, the tilers had built a stepped ramp against the rear of the furnace and lined the steps with tiles so that they could reach the top of their oven

10 Cistercian lay brothers of Meaux Abbey, Yorkshire, set up a tilery at North Grange, Meaux, to make mosaic tiles to pave the Abbey church between 1249 and 1269. Drawing of the probable form of their kiln based on fragments excavated in 1958.

11 In about 1240 an expert tiler constructed a kiln at Clarendon Palace, Wiltshire, to make two-colour segmental and rectangular tiles to pave the new chapel erected by Elias of Dyrham for Henry III. The excavated remains of this kiln have been reassembled and are exhibited in the Medieval Tile Room in the British Museum.

wall. This kiln measured about 2.28 m (7 ft 6 in) by 1.83 m (6 ft) internally, and each fire-box was 81.5 cm (2 ft 8 in) long. This kiln was superimposed upon the remains of an earlier, longer roof-tile kiln, of which the truncated remains were found protruding under the floor of the stoke hole of the upper kiln. The walls of both structures had been built of pre-fired roof tiles bonded together with clay.

The known kilns for firing floor tiles during the thirteenth and fourteenth centuries had ovens about 1.83 m (6 ft) square internally over only two furnace chambers. That excavated on the site of Clarendon Palace, Wiltshire, is typical. Those at Chertsey Abbey and Norton Priory were even smaller, possibly because the tilers needed to have more control over the temperature throughout their ovens when they were firing highly specialised tiles. The glazes used on floor tiles needed temperatures over 1000° centigrade to flux. Waste tiles recovered from the site of tileries at Ramsey Abbey and Lenton Priory and from the Leper Hospital at Burton Lazars had been rejected because of failure of the glaze to fuse: it remained on the surface looking like a buff to khaki slip. When examples of these tiles were fired to a tem-

perature of 1100° centigrade the glazes fused successfully, but at this temperature all the tile bodies were beginning to melt, demonstrating that they were unsuitable for glazed wares. These failures show what care the medieval tilers had to take in selecting clay for their tile bodies to avoid heavy financial loss. A rough pavement of these tiles from Burton Lazars is exhibited in the Medieval Tile Room at the British Museum.

Most tilers used wood for their fuel, although there is occasional evidence for the use of coal in northern England and lowland Scotland and there is a reference to the purchase of turf in East Anglia. These men were highly skilled in the management of their kilns, but even so there was a difference in oven temperature of 200° centigrade between the bottom at the front and the top at the back which made it almost inevitable that there was some overfired waste at the front and underfired waste at the back to be discarded after each firing. The medieval tilers had no scientific instruments with which to test the temperature of the ovens: the tilers had to use their experience and expertise to judge this by the colour of the tiles during firing, including those which made up the temporary oven roof. Indeed, the same empirical methods were used by the Wealden tilers, who were still manufacturing hand-made bricks and tiles until the 1960s. They walked about on the top of their ovens to assess the colour.

As has been mentioned, work in the tileries was seasonal. The kilns were fired only in the summer months of June, July and August. It is probable that each firing of the kiln took a week and that the work cycle was as follows:

Monday Tiles taken to the kiln and stacked on edge in tiers in the oven. If the stack reached the top of the oven wall, a temporary roof would be constructed.

Tuesday Stack completed if necessary and roof constructed. Slow-drying fire lit to drive off water still mixed in the fabric of the tiles. Oven temperature kept below 200° centigrade to avoid effects of too much steam causing expansion and bursting of tiles.

Wednesday Slow-drying fire maintained.

Thursday Forty-eight hours after lighting the slow-drying fire, temperature raised to 1000°–1100° centigrade. Final firing carried out with brushwood faggots to send flames right through the oven to clean the tiles. Mouths of the fire-boxes and apertures in the roof closed and kiln left to cool.

Friday Roof removed when oven temperature reduced to 200° centigrade; might be left until Saturday if necessary.

Saturday Oven unloaded, any waste discarded and rest of tiles stored.

Sunday A holy day.

Monday Weather permitting, cycle begins again.

The firing of these early kilns was heavily dependent on the weather: they had no roof over them and no hovel round them, therefore when it was really wet the ovens could not be loaded. We have documentary evidence for this. In the fourteenth century Battle Abbey owned a large tilery with over thirteen kilns at Knackholt (Naccolt), Wye, in Kent. Three times in the 1360s the monk in charge of this tilery could show only a small profit. He attributed this to three adverse factors: he had been unable to lease out many of the kilns because of the outbreak of the plague, in which many men had died; many others had been pressed into military service for the French war; and the weather had been so wet that even those kilns that had been leased could not be fully worked. It is interesting that the kilns in Battle Abbey's great tilery were leased to individual lay tilers.

It is probable that by the fifteenth century some kind of cover was constructed over the oven. At Mattens, Saffron Walden, Essex, just outside the moat surrounding the site of the manor house, a tile kiln was excavated. Traces of four possible supports for a light structure over it were found in close proximity to the outside of the kiln. Such a structure would have been very vulnerable to fire.

12 The furnace area of the Clarendon Palace tile kiln during excavation in 1937. It was probably in use between 1240 and 1244.

3 MONOCHROME DECORATED FLOOR TILES

The medieval tile-maker's craft embraced a wide range of products. That most constantly in demand was the plain roof tile; ridge tiles also were always necessary, and glazed roof tiles and glazed and decorated ridges were frequently required. From the middle of the thirteenth century paving tiles were in demand. At first these were only available to customers who were wealthy enough and had sufficient room for a tilery to be set up on their land, but commercial tileries were certainly in operation by the last quarter of the thirteenth century and possibly even earlier. It seems that anyone who could afford a professionally built house, whether in stone or timber, could afford to buy commercially produced floor tiles. The hall of a London merchant's house found during excavation in 1974 was laid mainly with decorated [13, 15] tiles and only a few plain glazed examples. The hall and solar of Clifton House, a merchant's [14] house in King's Lynn, Norfolk, probably from about the same date, was laid mainly with light and dark glazed tiles with some decorated examples. The number of medieval tile pavements known from domestic sites is increasing as more medieval dwellings are excavated. No decorated floor tiles have ever been found on the site of peasant houses, even in places where tiles were being made.

MONOCHROME RELIEF DECORATION
The decorated floor tiles found in the Chapter House at St Alban's Abbey date from the late [16] twelfth century and are so far the earliest post-

13 *Left* Tiles made by the 'Westminster' tilers possibly *c.*1260–1300, found *in situ*, paving the hall of a London merchant's house. Excavated in 1974.

14 *Opposite* Part of a pavement of tiles made by commercial tilers in the late thirteenth or early fourteenth century, laid in the merchant's solar at Clifton House, King's Lynn, Norfolk.

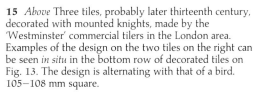

15 *Above* Three tiles, probably later thirteenth century, decorated with mounted knights, made by the 'Westminster' commercial tilers in the London area. Examples of the design on the two tiles on the right can be seen *in situ* in the bottom row of decorated tiles on Fig. 13. The design is alternating with that of a bird. 105–108 mm square.

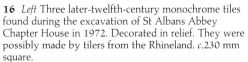

16 *Left* Three later-twelfth-century monochrome tiles found during the excavation of St Albans Abbey Chapter House in 1972. Decorated in relief. They were possibly made by tilers from the Rhineland. *c.*230 mm square.

17 Two designs based on the *Agnus Dei,* carried out in high modelled relief on monochrome tiles from Whitland Abbey, Dyfed, and Swineshead Abbey, Lincolnshire. 180 and 200 mm square.

19 *Overleaf* Commercial tilers known to have been operating at Bawsey in 1376 made these relief decorated tiles which were recovered from their waste heaps in 1930–31. The name THOMAS reversed can be seen on two tiles in the centre of the bottom row.

18 Three designs present on tiles from Bawsey, Norfolk: the first, asking prayers for the soul of Nicholas de Stowe, provides the one known date for when the tilers were operating; the second shows the debased heraldry that characterises their later designs; the third, the arms of de Toesne, was made for West Acre Priory, Norfolk. 100 mm square.

Conquest examples to which a reliable date can be assigned. They are decorated with designs in modelled relief. The decoration was applied with a carved wooden stamp when the tiles were leather-hard. Each tile was glazed a single colour: brown, dull green or black. When new, these glazes were iridescent and concentration in the depressions helped the decoration to stand out.

Tiles decorated in relief, both glazed and unglazed, are known to have been used on the Continent in the early medieval period, particularly in the Rhineland, and it is possible that the technique was introduced to St Alban's by Rhenish tilers. Such tiles continued to be produced in England until early in the eighteenth century. Many East Anglian tilers used this technique, probably influenced by trade contacts with the Rhineland across the North Sea. Some of them established a very flourishing industry at Bawsey outside King's Lynn in the last quarter of the fourteenth century.

It is possible that these tilers established themselves at Bawsey to fulfil an order for St Margaret's Priory there although there is no evidence of this. They certainly made tiles for West Acre Priory including designs with appropriate heraldry. They also made tiles for Castle Acre Priory where examples were found *in situ* in the nineteenth century. One of their designs includes the inscription 'Pray for the Soul of Nicholas de Stowe, Vicar'. His will was proved in Norwich Consistory Court in 1376. The stamp was probably carved in that year to decorate tiles made to cover his grave or surround his tomb in Snettisham church, where

he is known to have been buried. This provides us with one fixed date at which the tilers at Bawsey were active but we do not know when they began or finished working there. They ran a successful operation and distributed their tiles over a wide area in Norfolk and the hinterland of the Wash. They carved their stamps to produce decoration either in relief or counter-relief. It has been suggested that three different designers worked for the Bawsey tilery, the work of the third being of a poor quality. One of their designs consists only of the name THOMAS arranged in two rows of three letters but unfortunately the man who carved the stamp failed to cut THOMAS in reverse with the result that the name appears back-to-front on the tile. Nevertheless, many tiles of this design were produced and even used at such important places as Castle Acre Priory. He was by no means the only carver to make this mistake: numerous other examples of reversed designs can be recognised, particularly when heraldry is included in the decoration.

The Bawsey tilers used either a deep yellow or a near-black glaze, and some examples found *in situ* at Castle Acre were laid in alternate colours. The panel of Bawsey tiles exhibited in the British Museum has been reassembled in this way and includes fifteen different designs. The work of the first designer is simple and very competent and includes correct heraldry; that of the other two is inferior and includes false heraldry. Is it possible that the inferior stamps were cut by two of the tilers themselves, working in an unfamiliar medium to replace originals that had broken?

A roughly laid pavement of underfired tiles with defective glaze, dating from the late fifteenth or early sixteenth century, was found in 1913 on the site of the Leper Hospital at Burton Lazars, Leicestershire.

The last tilers to use relief decoration were working in Barnstaple from the later sixteenth to the early eighteenth century. The only known wooden stamp used for decorating the surface of a tile was found in North Walk Pottery, Barnstaple, and given to the British Museum in 1906. It is decorated with a fleur-de-lis in bloom flanked by the initials I B, and it has proved very

20 Part of a piece of paving dating to the fifteenth or sixteenth century and found in 1913 on the site of the Leper Hospital at Burton Lazars, Leicestershire. The tilers failed to obtain a high enough temperature to melt and fuse their glaze.

21 *Above* Tiles decorated in high relief, made by the post-medieval Barnstaple tilers. The tiles now form the pavement of the Sanctuary of Launcells Church, Cornwall.

22 *Left* This wooden tile stamp (centre), the only one known to survive, was used by the Barnstaple tilers to decorate the tile on the right. The stamp was found at North Walk Pottery, Barnstaple, in 1906, when the potters there used it to decorate the tile on the left.

informative. There is a large round depression in the middle of the back where the wood has been compressed and split, showing that the stamp was placed on the tile, a round-headed mallet put on top and struck one heavy blow with a hammer. This proves that the tilers did not mould their relief decoration, as has sometimes been suggested. The size of this stamp demonstrates that the tilers stamped the decoration when the tiles were already dry and leather-hard. We know the size of the fired tiles and can therefore deduce their size when they were formed. The wooden stamp is the intermediate size to which the formed tile would be reduced by the time it was leather-hard. The heavy use

to which the stamps were subjected eventually broke off projections, split them or broke them completely. The Barnstaple stamp had developed a crack near the bottom left corner and the tiler mended it with a large-headed iron nail, but even so he had eventually to discard it. A tile decorated with this stamp after it had been found in 1906 shows a ridge where the clay had penetrated the crack and an uneven surface where the wood had sprung. A tile in the British Museum bearing the same relief decoration was made before the stamp had cracked.

The Barnstaple tilers distributed their wares all over North Devon and into Cornwall, and also exported them to Ireland where a few have 23

23 *Left* two designs bearing the dates 1615 and 1708, the latter certainly used by the Barnstaple tilers. That including the name CARICFARGUS (top) was probably also used by them since other examples of their tiles have been found in Ireland. 150 and 143 mm square.

25 *Right* A repeating four-tile linear design of the fourteenth century used by the Repton tilers in Derbyshire and found on tiles associated with their kiln. Approx. 130 mm square.

24 *Above* Three linear designs of the fourteenth century, each impressed with a single stamp, present on tiles from Cheshire, Wales and Ireland, where some were certainly made. 120–122 mm square.

26 *Below* Linear decoration stamped by earlier fourteenth-century tilers with small individual stamps on mosaic shapes from Cambridge and Higham Ferrers, Northamptonshire.

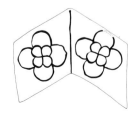

27 *Opposite* Part of a fourteenth-century panel with the line-impressed lion rampant shown in Fig. 24, laid with dark and light glazes. Found in 1971 during excavations at Swords Castle, Co. Dublin, and probably made by Irish tilers.

been found in the south and east. Their industry was undoubtedly subsidiary to the North Devon pottery industry which flourished at this time and exported wares to Ireland and North America.

LINE-IMPRESSED DECORATION

In the earlier part of the fourteenth century another type of decoration was introduced on monochrome tiles. This was carried out in line and generally impressed with a stamp. It seems that at first the tilers made a number of small stamps, each decorated with a single motif, rosettes, fleurs-de-lis and lions' faces being the most popular. These could be stamped in any combination on tiles of any size or shape but they were labour intensive as each stamp had to be picked up separately and carefully positioned on the tile. It was much simpler to make a stamp of the same size as the tile and that included all the required decoration. After the Black Death the tilers seem to have abandoned the use of separate stamps and to have confined themselves exclusively to the production of square tiles.

Line-impressed decoration was particularly popular throughout the Midlands and the North, where it was in use until early in the sixteenth century. Tilers in Chester established a flourishing industry in the later fourteenth century and continued into the fifteenth, and a comparable industry, using many of the same decorative designs, was established in Ireland where wasters found in Dublin and Drogheda demonstrate that the tiles were not imported from Chester. The tilers in both the English Midlands and Ireland used yellow and black glazes, and such examples as have been found in their original positions were laid alternately to give a chequered pattern. In the pavement excavated at Swords Castle, Co. Dublin, the glaze of the light-coloured tiles was streaked with a bright green. The tilers carrying out line-impressed decoration in Yorkshire in the late fifteenth and early sixteenth centuries used only a lead glaze applied directly to an oxidised tile body, and their pavements were all brown.

Another group of tiles, present in Staffordshire, is likely to date from the fifteenth century.

28 *Above* Six line-impressed tiles made by Midland tilers in the fourteenth century. Five are decorated with repeating single-tile designs, symmetrical on both axes so that the pavier could lay them any way round. The design on the sixth tile, which had been scored diagonally so that it could be broken into two triangles, was complete on a single tile. 120–133 mm square.

29 *Right* Tilers in the sixteenth century at Châteauneuf-en-Bray in Normandy used two line-impressed designs of Renaissance heads which have also been found on tiles in Sussex, probably made by local tilers. 118 mm square.

The designs are far less refined than any discussed so far and often include elements of relief and counter-relief. They were certainly applied with wooden stamps: not only are marks of cracks present but also marks of the grain of the stamp are sometimes visible in the bottom of the cavities. This suggests the use of a soft wood, in which the grain would easily be compressed. Moreover such stamps would break rather easily which would account for the many different versions of the designs that are present.

The last tilers known to have been using line-impressed decoration were working in Sussex, probably in the middle of the sixteenth century. Only two designs are known at present. These represent male heads in Renaissance helmets 29 and were impressed with the same stamps as a series of French tiles manufactured at Château-neuf-en-Bray. The tilers there, however, were using an iron-free body and a cobalt glaze, whereas the Sussex examples are apparently made of a usual red earthenware and glazed with a lead copper glaze, which suggests that they were made locally.

TILE MOSAIC
Some of the first decorative tile pavements to be laid in this country after the Norman Conquest were made in the Cistercian monasteries in Yorkshire. It is just possible that some were made at Byland Abbey at the end of the twelfth 30, 31 century, when there is a reference in the Monastic Chronicle to their tilery at Old Byland although it seems probable that this tilery was producing roof tiles rather than decorative mosaic floor tiles. It is possible to trace a sequence of mosaic pavements at these York-

30 Mosaic tiles of the mid-thirteenth century glazed either green or yellow, laid alternately in a circular arrangement of concentric bands. This exhibit in the British Museum was reassembled from tiles found loose on the site of Byland Abbey, Yorkshire, following arrangements still *in situ*. Probably the work of lay brothers, some of whose kiln-waste has been found there.

31 The tile mosaic pavement *in situ* in the south transept chapels in Byland Abbey church, showing the arrangement illustrated in Fig. 30.

shire houses by the decreasing thickness of the tiles and the increasing number of mosaic arrangements employed at each place. It seems probable that Fountains Abbey was the first to have such pavements: these were known to have been laid between 1220 and 1247. The tilers who made these mosaics almost certainly came from Cistercian houses on the Continent, where comparable pavements were also laid, but we do not know where they set up their tilery at Fountains. Some of their decorative arrangements have been relaid on the platform of the high altar of the Abbey Church where they may still be seen. These more complicated arrangements will have been used in the eastern arm and transepts, the most important areas of the church. The nave at Fountains was laid with arrangements of small tiles about 50 cm (2 in) square, glazed either black or yellow. The Fountains tiles are unusually thick, some as much as 50 cm (2 in), far thicker than was necessary for the surface area of the tile; this is one of the reasons to suppose that the work at Fountains came very early if not first in the series. Such unnecessary thickness was wasteful of clay and of space in the oven, and it is noticeable that the thickness of subsequent mosaics became progressively less.

Tilers certainly did make mosaic at Byland,

whether at the end of the twelfth century or nearer to the middle of the thirteenth, because waste mosaic tiles have been found on the abbey site. Unfortunately no trace of their kiln has been found: it is possible that their tilery at Old Byland was still in use, but the site of that has not yet been located. In the middle of the thirteenth century tilers were also making comparable mosaic pavements at Rievaulx Abbey and their tilery may well have been in Ryedale at a site now known as Tile Kiln Farm.

We know most about the tilers making mosaic pavements at Meaux Abbey, where the 32 Monastic Chronicle states that the church was paved during the abbacy of William, 1249 to 1269. Excavations on the site of the church have revealed many mosaics but no other type of tile, and it is clear that this mosaic pavement was that laid during William's abbacy, and that it was in use until the dissolution of the monastery. More mosaic arrangements have been recorded from Meaux than from any other of the northern monasteries. We also know from the Monastic Chronicle that Meaux Abbey had workshops at North Grange, half a mile distant from the precinct, and that these were operated by lay brothers. Excavations carried out at North Grange in 1932 and 1957 revealed that the tilery was situated there. The late thirteenth-

32 Drawing of a different arrangement of alternating green and yellow mosaic tiles in concentric circular bands. This reconstruction was based on tiles found during excavations on the site of Meaux Abbey church, where they are known to date from 1249 to 1269. See also Fig. 10.

century roof-tile kilns already mentioned overlay the very disturbed remains of a kiln for firing mosaic tiles. Fortunately, enough scattered pieces of kiln structure and tile waste were found to enable a reconstruction to be made of the kiln for firing tile mosaic and for the methods of manufacture to be deduced. The tilers rolled out slabs of clay on a sanded board and scored the mosaic shapes round templates. They then cut each shape free from the slab and pared down the sides of each tile so that the base was smaller than the surface. They made far fewer of the curved or elaborate shapes than of the small square tiles. Most of these that have been found were cut to shape before they were fired but remains of larger slabs were also found with the square shapes scored on the surface to a depth of

about one-third of the thickness of the tile. After such slabs had been fired they were placed face down, and a wooden bat was placed over them and struck one sharp blow. The slab usually split along its scored lines leaving the small square tiles separated, but sometimes it broke in the wrong place. The tilers clearly considered that the risk of such wastage was more than offset by the greater simplicity of stacking larger slabs into the oven.

The making and laying of these mosaic pavements was labour intensive. We have seen that the actual labour of making and firing the tiles was carried out by the lay brothers at Meaux. We do not know whether the designs for the arrangements were made by one of the monks, although it seems most likely that they were. It is, however, clear that the templates were passed on from one monastery to another. At each site the designer had to plan the division of the whole pavement into panels as well as to choose individual arrangements within the panels.

Hand-made ceramic tiles lose about one sixth of their formed size during the drying and firing processes but this shrinkage was uneven in the medieval kilns. The tiler who laid the pavement had always to work to the matrix of the largest tile, a task which was even more complicated in the laying of mosaic shapes than in the laying of more ordinary square tiles. Each panel was surrounded by tile borders. At Byland, where many still remain in position, these borders vary in width and it is possible that this variation was made by the pavier in order to compensate for variable shrinkage.

A panel of mosaic tiles from Rievaulx Abbey displayed in the British Museum Medieval Tile Room has been reassembled to demonstrate small areas of six different mosaic panels and eight borders. The pavier who laid these mosaic floors must have had drawings of the main arrangements in each panel to guide him. We do not know who was in charge of the work but he was probably a monk, perhaps the designer himself, and he would have to exercise frequent supervision. The pavier would start to lay each mosaic panel from the middle to enable him to compensate for any deviation from the

33 Panel assembled in the British Museum using loose tiles of the mid-thirteenth century from Rievaulx Abbey, Yorkshire. It shows a variety of the panel and border arrangements that the mosaic tile makers had used there.

expected size of the panel by altering the width of the borders. Laying the mosaic arrangements was clearly a much more expert and time consuming job than laying ordinary square tiles.

Mosaic tiles also took longer to make and to set in the oven. We know from the remains of kiln furniture recovered from the excavations at North Grange, Meaux, that temporary shelves were erected in the upper part of the oven on which curved shapes could be stacked. After the kiln had been fired the temporary shelves would have to be unloaded and removed in order to reach the rectangular tiles that were stacked on

the oven floor. All these operations would be time consuming. The lay brothers who carried out the work at Meaux would have received no wages and this would be so if the tilers at the other Cistercian houses were also lay brothers. Very little of this elaborate material has been found on any site where the work could not be done by lay brothers for nothing but their keep: the whole production was too expensive to have been carried out commercially. However, the sequence of dates and the multiplication of shapes suggest that the designer and the master tilers moved from abbey to abbey although each

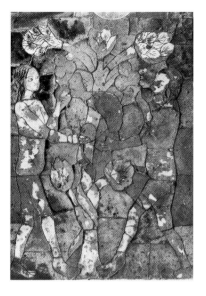

34 *Above* The most important surviving tile panel of *opus sectile in situ* before the altar in Prior Crauden's Chapel, Ely, *c.*1324. 1.15 × 0.85 m. It shows Adam and Eve and the Serpent with the forbidden fruit of the Tree of Knowledge. The shapes forming the picture are glazed yellow, olive green or reddish brown and the background shapes are black.
Left Photograph of the panel; *right* diagram of the shapes from which it was assembled.

35 *Below* One of sixteen *opus sectile* panels in Prior Crauden's Chapel, each depicting a lion, *c.*1324. Eight of the panels are large lions, four dexter and four sinister, eight are small lions both dexter and sinister. This illustration shows one of the large lions passant gardant sinister. 0.9 × 0.5 m.

generation must have trained its own successors because work went on for nearly a century.

UNUSUAL ELABORATE TECHNIQUES

In the earlier part of the fourteenth century a group of tilers were making some extremely complicated pavements which included several different elements of decoration. One of these, laid about 1224, is still in position in Prior Crauden's Chapel at Ely. A large panel in front of the altar depicts Adam and Eve with the serpent twined round the Tree of Knowledge. The east end of the pavement includes ten panels containing large lions, and there are four more at the west end. To make these figures the tilers must have followed the same methods as the earlier makers of plain tile mosaics, rolling out sheets of clay on a sanded table, scoring their shapes on it using templates and cutting out the shapes from the slab. These templates were reversible and the dexter and sinister lions are mirror images of each other. There the similarity ended because these shapes were not laid in alternating colours. Those forming the background of the panels were glazed black and those making up the figures were glazed yellow. This type of work is known as *opus sectile*. Further treatment was given to the components of the figures, particularly the heads. In the Adam and Eve panel the tilers drew the features by scoring the slip through to the body of the tile and they treated the eyes with a red clay. After the tiles were fired the eyes appeared dark brown and the scored lines a lighter brown in a yellow face. The eyes and tongues of the lions were treated in the same way, and locks of hair were scored on their bodies and legs. It is probable that these were scored through a stencil, but unfortunately the surface of the lions is so badly worn that it is not possible to make direct comparison of the position of the locks of hair on two comparable lions.

The areas surrounding these panels in the sanctuary are paved with various mosaic arrangements. Many of the mosaic components of the panels had linear decoration of rosettes or lions' faces impressed on them with small stamps. Four of the panels include a star-shaped figure, each composed of six five-sided tiles

36 Part of a line-impressed mosaic pavement, thought to date from *c.*1315, in the Sanctuary of Meesden Church, Hertfordshire, showing an earlier version of arrangements used at Ely and Old Warden Abbey, Bedfordshire.

scored to look as if it were made up of eight separate black tiles with a small triangular yellow tile inserted in the middle. This type of work is known as 'pseudo-mosaic'. Different pseudo-mosaic tiles are found at the north and south edges of the pavement, where the borders are made up of lozenge-shaped tiles decorated with birds and lions and square tiles decorated with lions and stags. Each figure was carried out in white slip and surrounded by a scored line to make it appear that yellow mosaic shapes were set in a black lozenge or square frame. As on the large lions, the tilers added a little linear detail to these figures.

The body of Prior Crauden's Chapel is paved with three panels of mosaic running west to east. The arrangements are based on contiguous and interlacing circles, those in the north and south panels being the same. The same stamps of rosettes and lions' faces were used to impress linear decoration on many components of the arrangements. This pavement is badly worn, but early illustrations reveal more detail than can now be seen. Comparable mixed techniques are known to have been used in pavements at Old Warden Abbey, Bedfordshire, and Norton Priory, formerly in Cheshire, their remains found during excavations.

37 *Above* Part of an elaborate mosaic arrangement, *c*.1324, including two forms of pseudo-mosaic, flanking the Adam and Eve panel in Prior Crauden's Chapel, Ely.

38 Pseudo-mosaic stag and lion, *c*.1324, in the north and south borders of the pavement in Prior Crauden's Chapel, Ely. 150 mm square.

THE TRING TILES

The most impressive tiles with slightly different linear decoration form a series associated with Tring Church in Hertfordshire, where most known examples were found. These illustrate scenes from the stories told in the Apochryphal Gospels of the Childhood of Christ, which were very popular in the fourteenth century. The method used here is known as *sgraffiato*. The tilers coated the whole surface of the tile with white clay, drew the outline of the figures and internal detail with a stylus through the white clay to the red body, and then removed the white clay from the background with a small gouge. The gouge used on the Tring tiles was 4 mm ($\frac{1}{4}$ in) wide. It is certain that this work was carried out by hand: there are a number of mistakes where the tiler scored a line which should not have been there, and on one tile he gouged away the white clay that should have been left on the body of one of the figures. The illustrations on these tiles resemble those in a manuscript (MS Selden Supra 38) in the Bodleian Library in Oxford, although they are not copies. It is probable that an artist made cartoons for the tilers to copy; no manuscript would be allowed anywhere near the messy clay and sand in a tilery.

The Tring tiles are the only known examples decorated in sgraffiato, but the various types of pseudo-mosaic and additional features added by hand are fairly widespread. These techniques are frequently associated with simpler line-impressed decoration but seem to have been used for a limited time, mainly in the earlier fourteenth century, after which they seem to have been abandoned because any additional handwork slows down production.

Experiments carried out at Norton Priory by Barry Johnson, who made replicas of the line-impressed mosaic found in the priory church there, demonstrated that it was possible to make these linear impressions in the usual way with wooden stamps. It has already been mentioned that projections frequently broke off wooden stamps when they began to wear out. In East Anglia and the Midlands the same stamps were used to decorate innumerable line-impressed tiles in many different places. These stamps

39 The child Jesus miraculously repairing a broken plough beam, carried out in *sgraffiato* on one of a series of tiles from Tring Church, Hertfordshire, earlier fourteenth century. The series is the work of a highly specialised tiler. Each tile 325 × 163 mm.

have their own minor idiosyncrasies which are recognisable on all tiles that were stamped with them. No wooden stamp could survive such intensive use, which suggests that metal stamps were used for this series. An experiment was carried out in the British Museum: the outline of a typical rosette was scored in the bottom of a clay mould which was then fired. Molten lead was then poured into the mould and left to cool. The result was a metal stamp with a linear rosette standing proud. This could be stamped on clay without the use of a release agent, and it left most satisfactory impressions. The tilers had the materials for making such stamps at hand in every tilery. The stamp could be set in a wooden block and would survive heavy use, and it could be passed from site to site. Perhaps the tilers themselves travelled from place to place taking the same metal stamps with them.

4 TWO-COLOUR DECORATED FLOOR TILES

In the second quarter of the thirteenth century a new type of decoration was introduced. The tiler stamped the decoration into the tile mainly in solid block and filled the cavities with white clay in a plastic state to produce a two-colour tile. It is thought that this technique was introduced into England from France, and it soon became the most popular type of decoration throughout England except perhaps in East Anglia. Such tiles were an integral part of the decoration of Gothic buildings, and millions must have been produced before they went out of fashion in the sixteenth century, when Renaissance architecture replaced Gothic.

Whereas in the past it was often thought that all tilers were attached to religious houses and ceased to operate at the time of the Dissolution of the Monasteries, more recent work has shown that most tilers were laymen and that they continued to produce their tiles for several decades afterwards.

CLARENDON AND THE WESSEX SCHOOL

The earliest two-colour decorated tiles for which we have dated documentary evidence were ordered by Henry III in 1237. He ordered a tiler at Westminster to make some tiles for St Stephen's Chapel if the marble for the floor there ran out. No trace of any of this pavement survives and we do not known if any such tiles were made. It is, however, clear that by this time a tiler capable of making high-quality tiles was working at Westminster. The earliest pavement of two-colour tiles for which we have both documentary and archaeological evidence is that made between 1240 and 1244 for the new chapel built for Henry III at Clarendon Palace by Elias of Dyrham. The furnace area of the kiln in which these tiles were fired was discovered during excavations in 1937. These remains were lifted in 1964 and later reassembled, and are now displayed in the Medieval Tile Room at the British Museum. The main feature of this pavement, of which a reassembled segment is exhibited above the kiln, was a large circular

arrangement of alternate bands of plain green glazed and decorated two-colour tiles.

The King's Clerks of Works were authorised to impress labour of all sorts for any royal building. Elias doubtless knew where he could find tilers who were expert in the new two-colour technique and brought them to Clarendon Palace; it is possible that they had been working at Beaulieu Abbey and St Denys' Priory in Hampshire. They were given a site between the great hall and the main kitchen in which to set up their tilery. An old ditch ran between the two buildings and they removed all the soil between this and the flint wall running beside the kitchen and there cut out for themselves a level platform on solid chalk. At the front of this platform they had a level area from which to stoke their furnace and uphill, at the back, there was a vertical chalk face. Unfortunately the platform proved slightly too narrow to accommodate the width of the kiln and they were obliged to scour the adjacent slope of the ditch and build it up with chalk blocks. On this they constructed their kiln, using waste glazed roof tiles from the local tilery to construct the lining of the furnace and the walls of the oven. They formed special voussoirs for the arches over the fire-boxes and the furnace chambers and built these into their structure without firing them first. Water was available from the well in the Great Court. The site of the other buildings of their tilery is not known; it is possible that they were able to use those already in existence for the roof-tile makers.

The master tiler's first commission was to make the tiles for a large circular arrangement of alternating bands of plain green glazed and decorated two-colour tiles. The decoration on two of these is also known from Beaulieu Abbey and St Denys' Priory, and it seems probable that he had already worked at both these sites and brought some at least of his stamps with him. The outermost decorated band contained an inscription, but as each letter was on a single tile and less than half of these have been recovered it

40

11, 12

40 *Overleaf* The tilers who, in 1240, set up the kiln at Clarendon Palace, Wiltshire, made the segmental tiles for a great circular arrangement in Henry III's new chapel. This segment was assembled from loose tiles recovered during excavations on the site and was augmented by plaster casts. See also Figs 11 and 12.

41 An arrangement of two-colour tiles in concentric circular bands, found in the cloisters at Muchelney Abbey, Somerset, in the 1880s and reset by the font in the parish church. Probably made in the mid thirteenth century by tilers who moved on into Somerset from Clarendon Palace.

is not possible to reconstruct the words. The pavier who laid these tiles must have had a diagram showing him the order in which the bands of decorated tiles were to be laid, but it was more difficult to distinguish between the components for the plain green glazed bands. In order that these should be correctly placed the tiler had scored assembly marks on the sides of the tiles. The tiles in the innermost and outermost bands have no assembly marks as they could not be confused, but the remainder are marked by a bevel, a sequence of nicks or Roman numerals. The only other tiles on which

assembly marks are known are components of some *opus sectile* at Old Warden Abbey. At the same time as he was making the segmental tiles for the circular arrangement, he was also making some decorated oblong tiles for use as borders, tiles to be set vertically to face risers of steps and square tiles for other parts of the paving of the new building. All his tiles are very well made and the decoration is carried out in deep inlay. This technique presented difficulties because the two different coloured clays tended to shrink at different rates during drying and firing, and if the white clay shrank too much cracks appeared

42 Colour plate of the pavement of Salisbury Cathedral Chapter House, published by Henry Shaw in 1858. It shows the remarkable way in which the tilers used the octagonal shape of the building to devise this beautiful arrangement of their panels. They may have been the same craftsmen who made the tiles for the Cathedral, or possibly their successors, because the Chapter House was not begun until after the Cathedral was finished in 1258. This thirteenth-century pavement has been replaced by a nineteenth-century replica.

round it and it sometimes fell out of the cavities. Tests carried out on comparable inlaid tiles used at Winchester at that time revealed that the tilers there had added some body clay to their white clay in an attempt to equalise shrinkage, but it is not known whether the tilers at Clarendon did the same. When the makers of such inlaid tiles had stamped the cavities and filled them with the white clay they would put a wooden bat over the surface and hammer it down to consolidate the two clays. They would then remove any surplus white clay and pare carefully round the edges of the inlay with a knife to define the edge of the decoration more precisely.

A few isolated segmental tiles that do not belong to the arrangement from the King's Chapel at Clarendon Palace suggest that these tilers made two more circular pavements, but it is not known whereabouts in the Palace they

were used. This phase of tiling was completed by 1244, the superstructure of the kiln was thrown down into the furnace and a salting house built over the site. The tilers dispersed, one at least travelling to Somerset where the remains of two circular arrangements resembling, but not identical with, those at Clarendon were found in the cloister at Muchelney Abbey in the 1880s and relaid in the parish church. A few isolated segmental tiles of the same type have been found during excavations at Glastonbury.

Excavations carried out at Nash Hill, Lacock, Wiltshire, in 1971 revealed the remains of two pottery kilns, a roof-tile kiln and a more sophisticated structure firing decorated two-colour floor tiles, thought to have begun operating towards the end of the thirteenth century. Among the waste floor tiles were some decorated with stamps that had been used at Clarendon, designed to face the risers of steps. This suggests that a successor to the Clarendon tilers was working at Nash Hill and that he still possessed a few of the Clarendon stamps. Those used to decorate tiles for risers would have been used far less frequently than those that decorated square tiles needed to cover a whole floor, and we may assume that any of those that he had had from Clarendon had long ago worn out.

Another phase of tile paving was undertaken at Clarendon in Wiltshire in the early 1250s. The tiles used for this were the same as those being made for the paving of the new cathedral at Salisbury, and it is probable that they were made there since there is no sign that they were manufactured on the palace site. These tiles are smaller than those made for the King's Chapel, and the decorative designs are less emphatic. They belong to a series that was widespread in Wiltshire, Hampshire and adjacent counties and are generally known as the products of the Wessex school.

One further series of tiles was later manufactured at Clarendon itself, where waste heaps were located in 1939. These were made of a very distinctive clay containing haematite and magnetite. When the clay was in flux the iron particles ran together leaving the fired body a

44 Detail of Queen Philippa's chamber pavement (Fig. 43) showing pairs of lions and griffins, common to the Wessex school.

43 The remaining west end of a pavement of inlaid tiles lifted in 1957 from the ground floor chamber of Queen Philippa's new apartments at Clarendon Palace, Wiltshire. Except in the centre panel, almost all the tiles occupy their original position. The pavement dates from 1250–2 and was made by the tilers then working in Salisbury, producing the tiles to pave the new cathedral. Each tile 140–145 mm square.

45 *Above* The three elements of a hunting scene in the intrusive panels in Westminster Abbey Chapter House paved by 1258. Each tile 190–195 mm square.

46 *Right* Westminster Abbey Chapter House border designs of pikes set alternately dexter and sinister. *Top and middle* 1250s; *bottom* 1860s. 210 × 95 mm.

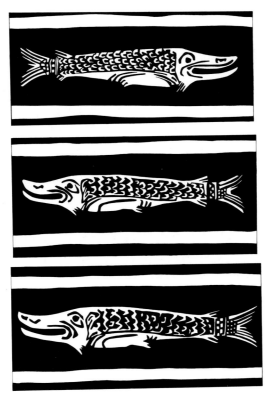

pale colour with small, dark, red-brown patches. This made a poor contrast with the white inlay and, although examples are known from other sites in Wiltshire, this industry seems to have died out fairly soon.

WINCHESTER, CHERTSEY AND WESTMINSTER

At much the same time that one group of tilers was working for Elias of Dyrham at Clarendon Palace, another group was employed on the King's work at Winchester and Westminster. The remarkable pavement that they made for the Chapter House at Westminster Abbey is still there although much restored in the 1860s. We know that this pavement was laid before 1258 because in that year Henry III ordered that the tiles left over from it should be used in St Dunstan's Chapel. The tiles were laid in panels running from west to east across the octagonal building, each panel being laid with tiles of one design only. This regular arrangement is interrupted in two of the panels in the south part of the floor, where rows of tiles decorated with figural scenes and inscriptions, quite different from those in the rest of the floor, are laid. Is it possible that these were left over from some grander pavement in Westminster Palace?

At Winchester tilers were making a mosaic with two-colour tiles, including large circular

45, 46
47, 48

47 Part of a panel of inlaid tiles, laid by 1258, in Westminster Abbey Chapter House, illustrating Aesop's fable of the cock and the fox. Made by expert tilers known, from documentary evidence, to have been working at Westminster for Henry III. 160 mm square.

48 *Opposite* A seated queen holding her falcon. One of the designs, used on a tile made by Minten and Co. in 1842, in the intrusive panels in Westminster Abbey Chapter House, laid by 1258.

49 Two circular pictures fired *c.*1250 in four pieces, showing Richard I and Saladin, set in an elaborate two-colour background. The tiles are part of a series illustrating combats; they are from the site of Chertsey Abbey, Surrey. 0.8 × 0.5 m.

49 emblemata decorated with scenes of personal combat. Only a few fragments have been found, reused as rubble beneath the presbytery steps, and it is not known whether they came from the cathedral or the palace. It is more likely that such decoration was designed for the palace, but comparable tiles might also have been used in the cathedral. A large number of tiles decorated with these combat scenes have been found on the site of Chertsey Abbey in Surrey, where they form part of a group of brilliantly decorated two-colour tiles made during the thirteenth century and known collectively as Chertsey tiles.

The circular tiles decorated with combat scenes were fired in four quarters and set in a mosaic background. The makers of the Chertsey tiles subsequently reduced the amount of labour when they made a further series decorated with scenes from the romance of Tristram and Isolde: 52,55, these roundels were fired in one piece and set in 57 square frames fired in four sections. These, the most famous of the Chertsey tiles, are technically remarkable. In the last decade of the thirteenth century some of the same Tristram pictures were used at Halesowen Abbey, then in Worcestershire, and it may be supposed that at least one tiler went there from Chertsey taking his stamps with him. At the same time another of the Chertsey tilers seems to have gone to Hailes Abbey in Gloucestershire, taking with him other stamps from Chertsey.

45

The detail of the decoration on the Chertsey tiles is so intricate that it is unlikely to have been 50, 51 reproduced on so many examples in different places by hammering the stamp into a leather-hard tile in the usual way: the many small projections would soon have broken off. It seems probable that these tilers placed their stamps in the base of a mould and pressed wet clay down on to them. Evidence for this is supplied by the decoration of the frames in which these roundels were set. The corner foliate decoration is the same in all Chertsey examples, although different terminals were used at Halesowen and yet others at Hailes. One quarter of the circular band surrounding the picture was included in each corner tile. Many different inscriptions and decorative motifs were used in this circular band. This suggests that the stamp for the foliate corner was fixed in the mould and that separate small stamps decorated with letters, crowns, various grotesques and foliate scrolls could be individually slotted into the band in the mould. These stamps might have been made of metal, but hardwood should survive wet moulding satisfactorily. The tiles would have to be left to dry in the mould and this process would consequently be slow and expensive.

50 and 51 *Left* Heads of a king and a lady on tiles only 49 mm in diameter, examples of the most intricate work achieved by the Chertsey tilers, *c.*1250. Possibly used in the same mosaic arrangement in Fig. 49.

52 *Above* Design used by the Chertsey tilers, *c.*1260s–80s, showing Tristram playing his harp to King Mark; one of those illustrating the Romance of Tristram and Isolde. Diameter 235 mm.

The Chertsey tilers made another series of smaller circular pictorial tiles decorated with signs of the Zodiac, Labours of the Months and 53, 5 courtly scenes, all very popular subjects in the thirteenth century. At first these were fired separately and set in square frames fired in one piece; later the circular picture and its frame were fired together as one tile. These also provide evidence of wet moulding. Where such a tile has broken it is clear that a lump of finely prepared clay was pressed over the circular picture and the rest of the mould filled with clay of a coarser texture that was sufficient to take the simpler foliate decoration of the frame. The tiler who went to Hailes Abbey took with him some at least of the stamps for this series.

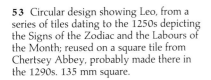

53 Circular design showing Leo, from a series of tiles dating to the 1250s depicting the Signs of the Zodiac and the Labours of the Month; reused on a square tile from Chertsey Abbey, probably made there in the 1290s. 135 mm square.

54 A roundel showing a man weeding, from the series depicting the Labours of the Month (referred to in Fig. 53). A good example of the skill of the tilers in inlaying small intricate decoration. Diameter 120 mm.

55 *Opposite* Four roundels, set in square frames, illustrating the Romance of Tristram and Isolde. The Chertsey tilers, *c.*1260s–80s, had reduced the complexity of the background but the work in the pictures is still intricate.

The tiler at Halesowen also made tiles with designs appropriate to the site, including a circular tile decorated with the figure of a seated abbot holding a crosier in his left hand and the model of a building in his right. A new stamp was cut for the frame based on the Chertsey foliate scroll but with vine leaves instead of stiff-leaf terminals, and other stamps were cut with grotesques similar to those used at Chertsey. New stamps were also cut for the circular band decorated with an inscription, stating that Abbot Nicholas gave this work to the Mother of God. This design must ante-date the Abbot's death in January 1299.

At both Chertsey and Halesowen the tilers further simplified their work by using their pictorial circular stamps on square tiles. At Chertsey the pictures were flanked by rather poorly-drawn architectural borders designed to be used with a new series of panels depicting a king, a queen, an archbishop and a Crucifixion, each beneath a canopy and flanked by better architectural borders. Waste tiles of this series were associated with the kiln discovered and excavated on the site of Chertsey Abbey in 1922. The architecture they depict suggests a date in the 1290s, and they may be associated in some way with memorials to Eleanor of Castile. Although these panels were clearly designed to be set vertically, the wear on the known examples shows that they had been used on floors. A few fragments found under the presbytery steps in Winchester Cathedral indicate that these panels had also been used there. Examples of the archbishop tiles only, both in their original form and debased copies, are known from churches in Hampshire and West Sussex. This suggests that one of the tilers working at Chertsey moved down to Winchester and went on again, possibly to set up for himself, taking the archbishop stamps with him.

The Chertsey tilers made large numbers of the more ordinary square paving tiles of which the decoration, both in design and execution, was of a remarkably high standard. The work of these craftsmen was decoratively and technically better than that of any other medieval tilers known either in France or England. We may suppose that cartoons were made for

56 *Left* One of four panels of the 1290s depicting a king, a queen, an archbishop and a crucifixion, all under architectural canopies. This panel, reassembled in the British Museum with loose tiles from the site of Chertsey Abbey, shows the archbishop. The Chertsey tilers fired the tiles of this series in the kiln discovered in the precinct and excavated in 1922. 800 × 220 mm.

57 *Opposite, left* One of the designs illustrating the Romance of Tristram and Isolde, showing the porter opening the gate of the castle. Used on circular tiles in the 1260s–80s, reused by the Chertsey tilers in the 1290s, adapted for use on square tiles with architectural borders linking it with the new panels and fired in the same kiln. See also Fig. 55. Diameter 232 mm; 228 mm square.

58 *Opposite, right* Part of a pavement of square tiles, late thirteenth century, found *in situ* in the chancel of the Abbey church at Halesowen, West Midlands. The tiles were probably made locally by the tilers who made the Chertsey-type tiles there. The beautiful design of the bird on the left was also used at Winchester Castle.

59 *Above* The pavement of the old refectory at Cleeve Abbey, Somerset, conserved *in situ*. The heraldic tiles were designed to celebrate the marriage of Edmund of Cornwall to Margaret de Clare in 1271/2.

61 *Above* Part of a pavement in the new eastern arm of Hailes Abbey church, Gloucestershire, consecrated in 1278; found during excavations in 1967. The inlaid tiles are decorated with specially designed heraldry connected with Richard and Edmund of Cornwall, their wives and others. It is probable that they were made locally by tilers employed by the Clerk of Works in charge of the new building.

60 *Left* These designs, showing the arms of England (top), Poitou (left) and de Clare (right), were derived from those at Cleeve Abbey (Fig. 59) and were used on tiles in Wells Cathedral in the late thirteenth century. Each tile approx. 135 mm square.

them by one of the king's painters, probably basing them on manuscript illustrations, that the designs were carved on wooden stamps by one of the king's master carvers, and that the tilers applied these to their clays with consummate technical skill.

Tiles decorated with non-pictorial Chertsey and Westminster designs are known from a number of other sites in London and Surrey and influenced the designs used by other groups of tilers in the south-east.

CLEEVE ABBEY

When Edmund of Cornwall, Henry III's nephew, married Margaret de Clare in 1271 he had heraldic decoration designed to celebrate his marriage and thus another series of designs was added to the stock of the Wessex tilers. It is not known where the tilers first made and laid these tiles, but a complete pavement remains in position in the old refectory at Cleeve Abbey in Somerset. The high table end of the floor is paved with sixteen-tile groups of three heraldic designs: the Royal Arms, the Arms of Poitou (Edmund's father, Richard of Cornwall, had been made Count of Poitou when he came of age) and the Arms of Clare. These tiles are large, about 200 mm (8 in) square. The rest of the room is paved with smaller tiles, some of which are decorated with Richard of Cornwall's double-headed eagle.

The tilers who made these tiles went on to other sites in Somerset, including Glastonbury, taking their stamps with them and also designing smaller versions of the same heraldry. They used slightly different large versions at Amesbury Abbey, which suggests that by the time they were working there the original stamps had been broken. The presence of some of their designs on waste tiles at Nash Hill suggests that this was one of their tileries. It is interesting that they were working with someone who still possessed a few Clarendon stamps. These tilers and apparently all those of the Wessex school continued to introduce their white clay as plastic inlay.

HAILES ABBEY

At about the same time as the Cleeve tiles were

being made, another group of tilers was working for Edmund of Cornwall at Hailes Abbey. In 1270/1 Edmund bought a relic of the Holy Blood and presented it to the Cistercian abbey at Hailes that had been founded by his father. A large extension of the eastern arm of the church built to house the shrine containing this relic was completed in 1278. The whole of this new work was paved with tiles designed especially for it, and we may suppose that Edmund's clerks pressed tilers into service and that they set up their tilery on the site, although this has not been located. Most of the decoration is heraldic and includes the royal arms and those of Richard of Cornwall as Count of Poitou and as King of the Romans, and also those of Richard's three wives. Edmund also included the arms of his wife and those of the families whose estates he had acquired. Each panel in the floor was laid with tiles of one design but, as has already been mentioned, variety was added by laying oxidised and reduced examples alternately.

The work of the tilers at Hailes was finished by 1278, and it seems that they moved on to make similar tiles elsewhere. The fabric of their tiles always looks the same: they added a liberal filler of sand to their body clay and insured that their tiles dried and fired easily by stabbing the backs with a scatter of small, round holes made with an implement shaped like a sharpened pencil. Their inlay is hard and very white and often stands a little above the surface of the tile on examples that are not very worn, and it may be pure kaolinite — indeed, as these tilers had originally worked for Edmund of Cornwall, they could have established links with the china clay producers of that county. Tiles with these characteristics are present in Oxfordshire, Bedfordshire, Buckinghamshire, Northamptonshire, Leicestershire and Warwickshire. It is interesting, however, that of the stamps used at Hailes only the royal arms has so far been recognised on any of their tiles in these areas. This would suggest that, contrary to usual practice, Edmund had kept the rest of his designs exclusive.

No kiln associated with this industry either at Hailes or elsewhere has yet been found, nor do we know whether this group of tilers worked

62 Panel of six of the inlaid tiles made for the new eastern arm of Hailes Abbey church in the 1270s, decorated with six of the heraldic designs. Each tile approx. 135 mm square.

63 Panel of nine tiles of the 'stabbed Wessex' series, derived from those used at Hailes Abbey in the 1270s; initially made by some, at least, of the same tilers and still produced by their successors until the 1330s.

from one centre or whether they moved from place to place. Waste tiles of this type have been found at Chetwode Priory in Buckinghamshire, suggesting that they had worked there at some time. Their industry is among the earliest commercial ventures known in England, and it 63 seems to have persisted at least until the 1330s when their tiles were being used in the church of St Peter-in-the-East in Oxford.

'WESTMINSTER'
A series of tiles that have been called 'Westminster' because they were first recognised in the pavement of the muniment room at Westminster Abbey, where they still remain, can now be dated to the middle part of the thirteenth century because examples have been found associated with a datable phase of the timbers of the Thamesside quays. Tiles of this type are also present in St Faith's Chapel in Westminster Abbey. It is not known where they were made, although this was possibly in the London area. They were distributed apparently along Watling Street as far as Warwickshire. These are probably the worst made medieval tiles ever to be commercially successful, although even poorer examples were produced elsewhere in small quantities, probably experimentally and for purely local use. The designs include a 13, 15 mounted knight, a bird, a shield of arms, a foliate cross and various fleurs-de-lis. The tiles are quite thick and the stamped cavities deep, but the surface treatment was inadequate. It appears that the white clay was inserted as a very thick slip but that instead of cutting off the surplus white and body clays from the top of the tile, the tiler merely wiped off the surplus white clay, covered the top with a bat and hammered it down, with the result that the surplus body clay rose up a little during firing. The surface of the tiles is rarely flat and on the same tile some of the decoration may be smudged where the white clay has overflowed the cavities, while other cavities are inadequately filled, leaving hollows in the surface. The first piece of decorated tile pavement to be found on a domestic site in the City of London was laid with these tiles. It was in a house just upstream from London Bridge, discovered during excavations on the site of Seal House in 1974.

DANBURY
The most complete excavation of a medieval tilery was carried out at Danbury near Chelmsford in Essex in 1974, where two kilns, two 7 workshop areas, a possible heated drying shed, two ovens for the preparation of lead ash for the glaze, a house, perimeter ditches and numerous pits were found. Some of the decorative designs on waste tiles found here were derived from those of the Westminster-Chertsey group, suggesting that possibly one of the Danbury tilers had been trained at Westminster or Chertsey, although apparently he possessed none of the stamps used there. He and his associates ran their tilery at Danbury for several decades at the end of the thirteenth and the beginning of the fourteenth centuries. Two other tileries were working in Essex at much the same time at Stebbing and Mill Green. The Danbury tilers seem to have set up their tilery as a commercial venture and their tiles were widely distributed in central Essex. They economised in the use of expensive white clay for decoration by making the cavities very shallow. It is not certain how they introduced the white clay, although it was possibly as a fairly thick slip. Various other methods have been suggested but it seems improbable that any of them could be carried out satisfactorily with medieval materials.

It is not known exactly when the Danbury tilers went out of business, but at least one of them seems to have moved to Hertfordshire, probably originally to St Albans. A very distinc- 64 tive, neatly made series of tiles is known from here and other sites in the county. Here again the tilers economised in the use of white clay, but the appearance of their tiles is different from those from Danbury. The area of decoration is surrounded by very sharp lines and the surface of the white clay is slightly below that of the tile. Some of their designs are identical with those on tiles made at Penn in Buckinghamshire, and it is possible that a Hertfordshire tiler moved there with his stamps.

64 Four tiles from St Albans Abbey, Hertfordshire, early fourteenth century; part of a distinctive series present in the county. Probably made by tilers who had worked in Essex, some of whom seem later to have moved on to Penn, Buckinghamshire. Each tile approx. 125 mm square.

the mosaic arrangements are composed of rectilinear shapes which were scored on thin rectangular tiles and separated after firing. The mosaic in the corona of St Thomas in Canterbury Cathedral is of an off-white fabric comparable to that of the French examples; indeed, it is even possible that these tiles were imported. The components of similar mosaics in Rochester Cathedral are made of the usual English red earthenware, as indeed are the two-colour decorated square tiles from Tyler Hill.

These tilers produced a good, hard, high-fired fabric over which the glaze appeared purplish-brown and cream. Their distinctive tiles are distributed widely in east Kent and parts of Essex, but their decorated two-colour floor-tile industry was probably fairly short-lived: the main products of the Tyler Hill kilns were roof tiles and roof furniture.

TYLER HILL, CANTERBURY

From the mid-thirteenth to the mid-fourteenth century there was a flourishing pottery industry on Tyler Hill, to the north of Canterbury, where a large number of pottery kilns and four tile kilns have been found. It is possible that the tilers who allied themselves with the potters working here came from France in the later thirteenth century, since their work is not in the mainstream of development in the south-east of England. Their decorated tiles were used in Canterbury Cathedral and St Augustine's Abbey in conjunction with a type of small mosaic known from the region around Paris. All

PENN

The best known and most successful of the commercial tileries was that established at Penn in Buckinghamshire in the fourteenth century. The first known documentary mention of this tilery is in 1344, when roof tiles were paid for, but decorated floor tiles were also already being made there. In the Subsidy Roll for 1332 two tilers and one pavier were listed among the taxable inhabitants of Penn and Taplow. They were Henry Tyler, Symon the Pavyer and John the Tyler. All were farmers as well as tilers and

65 Three designs present on tiles made at Penn where the tilers established a highly successful commercial enterprise lasting from the 1330s to the 1380s. Their tiles suggest three phases of production, illustrated by these three designs and each less competent than the last. 118, 110, 106 mm square.

66 Part of a pavement of tiles made in the mid fourteenth century by the Penn tilers during their main, middle, period of mass production; found *in situ* during excavation of the church of Elstow Abbey, Bedfordshire, in 1968.

were already prosperous: between them they were assessed to pay almost as much tax as the lord of the manor and his mother. Their tilery was in production at least until the 1380s, probably run by three generations of tilers. A Penn tiler named Robert, perhaps a son of Henry or John, was paid for roof tiles in 1353 and floor tiles in 1356. During the whole period that decorated floor tiles were made at Penn, but particularly after the Black Death in 1349, Penn tiles were bought by Royal Clerks of Works and therefore appear in the Royal accounts.

There seem to have been three main phases of production. During the first, which probably lasted until the Black Death, the tiles were slightly larger and better made than those produced later; a few of the designs included inscriptions, heraldry and human figures and needed to be set the right way round. The second phase was the main period of production, probably lasting from the Black Death until the 1360s or 1370s. During this time most of the churches and other important buildings in Buckinghamshire and neighbouring counties and along the Thames Valley as far as London were paved with Penn tiles. During the earlier period the tilers sold their products at six shillings per thousand at the kiln and the

purchasers paid separately for transport, which sometimes cost nearly as much as the tiles themselves. We do not know whether the carters and boatmen who provided transport were connected with the tilers or worked independently.

It is clear from the Subsidy Roll that at least one pavier, the man who actually laid the pavements, was connected with the tilery: this was Symon the Pavyer, who, as we have seen, was grouped with the two tilers for purposes of tax. The property on which this tax was assessed included stocks of lime which was needed not for the manufacture of the tiles but for the mortar in which the tiles were laid.

In 1352 one Elias the Tiler laid eight thousand tiles in the Chapter House of the Canons in Windsor Castle. These tiles cost six shillings and six pence per thousand: the Penn tilers had raised their prices after the Black Death. Many other Penn tiles were purchased for Windsor Castle at this time, but only those laid in the Aerery in 1354 still remain in position.

Each master tiler probably had several assistants. Elias and his mates were not paid a day wage but contracted to do the job for a fixed sum. This was a common method of payment in the later Middle Ages and meant that it was in the interests of the workmen to finish quickly, although the work had to be done well because it was then inspected by the Clerk of Works before the tilers were paid. We do not know whether Elias was a colleague or successor of Symon the Pavyer, or whether he hired himself and his mates to the Royal Clerk of Works independently. He may even have been pressed for this service: on 22 May 1350 three Royal Clerks of Works were empowered to press tilers for work in Westminster Palace and the Tower of London, and also to collect tiles from Penn.

Arnold Brocas was the clerk in charge of work at the Royal Palace at Sheen between September 1384 and February 1388. During this time he paid fifteen shillings to Katherine Lyghtefoote of Old Windsor for two thousand decorated tiles to pave the King's bathroom. We are not certain whether the tiles used at Sheen came from Penn but it is highly probable. If they were Penn tiles it would suggest that Katherine Lyghtefoote was a 'middleman'. Earlier, in 1366/7, Robert Herewyk, pavier, had been paid an agreed sum for paving the kitchen and new chamber at Sheen. Unfortunately, after his queen, Anne of Bohemia, died there in 1394, Richard II had the palace demolished so that it is impossible to relate these accounts to any surviving material evidence. Geoffrey Chaucer acquired a thousand tiles from the demolished palace for St George's Chapel, Windsor, but the account roll does not state whether these were floor or roof tiles.

In the nineteenth century many Penn tiles were recovered from the site of Baynard's Castle in the City of London, and records survive of work undertaken there from 1361 to 1366, when new buildings were erected to house the king's Great Wardrobe. Thirteen thousand tiles were bought from Hugo Reyn at ten shillings a thousand and John Lane was paid for paving a chamber called the Tailors' and another called the Skinners' in the King's Wardrobe. It is almost certain that John Lane used some of the Penn tiles bought from Hugo Reyn. In 1366 Bernard Cook, one of the king's clerks, bought fifteen thousand paving tiles from John Lightfot for work at Eltham Palace. Was Katherine Lyghtefoote carrying on a family business after the death of her father or her husband? Between 1384 and 1388 Henry Yevele, the king's mason, was paid eight shillings for a thousand decorated tiles called Penn tiles and two shillings and five pence for 296 tiles called Penn tiles, bought and used by him to pave and repair the pavement below the private garderobe of the king in the Tower of London. The tilers had raised their prices again.

These tiles bought in the 1380s may be identified with the products of the third phase of manufacture at Penn. They are even smaller than those of the second phase, frequently over-fired, and the decoration is inferior in both design and execution. There are no known later records specifying the use of Penn tiles and the decorated floor-tile industry there had probably come to an end by 1400, although doubtless the manufacture of roof tiles continued.

The success of the Penn tilers was due partly to the good quality of all but their latest wares and partly to their business ability. Their tiles were smaller than most that had been made previously, which meant that they could make more from one cartload of clay, fire more at one loading of the oven and get more of the finished tiles into one cart. As they sold the tiles at a price per thousand, their products were more profitable than they would have been had each tile been larger. They had succeeded in evolving a size which was not too small for the pavier to lay, although the thickness of their tiles was in fact rather less than was satisfactory for the surface area and many of their tiles are slightly dished, with the result that they wore at the corners. It is noticeable that in the second and third stages of production most of the single tile designs are symmetrical on both axes so it did not matter which way round they were laid, and the four-tile patterns are based on circular bands which demonstrate very clearly how the fours were to be set. Both devices made the pavier's work easier and quicker. The Penn tilers had thus devised a product which could be sold at an affordable price and leave a margin of profit for themselves. The fact that the Royal Clerks of Works used Penn tiles almost exclusively in the south-east for five or six decades speaks for the quality of these products.

67 Panel of six tiles, c.1320–30, from the site of Ulverscroft Priory, Leicestershire. They were made by tilers who set up their kiln on the site of the great commercial pottery at Chilvers Coton, Warwickshire. Each tile approx. 120 mm square.

LITTLE BRICKHILL

In the late fifteenth and early sixteenth centuries tilers at Little Brickhill on Watling Street in Buckinghamshire were producing two-colour 68 tiles commercially. The site of their kiln has been excavated. The fabric of their tiles was well fired and satisfactory, but the decoration was remarkably primitive. The majority of their designs were reproduced in outline instead of the more usual block, the outlines reserved in body clay and the white clay run over the rest of the surface. Most of the designs, for which the tilers may have cut their own stamps, are based on fleurs-de-lis, Catherine wheels and circular bands, some with illegible inscriptions. The glazes often contained a small admixture of copper or brass, with the result that the tiles were very light and bright with a varied yellow and light green colour. During work at Milton Keynes two pavements laid with these tiles were found, one in the chapel of Bradwell Priory and the other in the nave of the church at Great Linford. These show that, in spite of the inferior designs with which they were decorated, these tiles made a bright and pleasing pavement and were sold in Buckinghamshire and neighbouring counties, distribution being mainly by way of Watling Street.

WARWICKSHIRE

The Chertsey-type tiles made and used in Halesowen Abbey in the last decade of the thirteenth century and on into the early fourteenth were succeeded there by some small, square tiles, including one design known from Winchester Castle and probably made by the same group of tilers. Later, possibly about 1320, some even smaller tiles were used at Halesowen; these are known also from Lilleshall Abbey in Shropshire and Chilvers Coton in Warwickshire. 67 At Chilvers Coton they were associated with one of two tile kilns found on the site of a very large pottery. The decorative designs used at all three sites were mainly the same, but fabric and glaze were sufficiently different to suggest that they were made at three different places and that the tilers moved from one to the other. Certainly at Chilvers Coton the tilers were able to set up their kiln at a well established pottery

68 *Right* The commercial tilers working at Little Brickhill in Buckinghamshire in the late fifteenth and early sixteenth centuries used these three rather incompetent repeating four-tile designs on some of their well-made tiles. 112–117 mm square.

69 Three versions of a castle and fleur-de-lis border design, possibly associated with Eleanor of Castile, *c.*1290–1310. That on the left, probably the earliest, was used by the tilers at Chertsey. The middle version is known on tiles from Hailes and Halesowen Abbeys, made by the tilers presumed to have moved there from Chertsey. The Warwickshire tilers used the third version on some of their products known from Kenilworth Abbey and Maxstoke Priory. 162–172 × 60–75 mm.

where the raw materials they required were already present. The products of the second, later, Chilvers Coton kiln were entirely different and were probably first made for use at Ulverscroft Priory in Leicestershire around 1320–30.

Another Warwickshire tile industry was already centred in Coventry, where the tilers are the only ones known to have been allowed to form a guild. These tilers were using some of the Chertsey-type stamps used at Halesowen, as well as other later ones, decorated with grotesques, used at Hailes Abbey, and it seems likely that this industry was established by tilers who had worked at those places. The remains of a kiln, found in Stoke Park, Coventry, in 1911, yielded wasters of thirteenth-, fourteenth- and early fifteenth-century date, but the majority of Coventry-type tiles appear on stylistic grounds to belong to the late thirteenth and first half of the fourteenth century.

NOTTINGHAM

In Nottingham another tile industry seems to have been associated with the well-established potteries of the area and perhaps again, as at Chilvers Coton, tilers occasionally took the opportunity to set up their kilns at a pottery, where most of the raw materials would be available.

It is thought that the Nottingham tilers began production early in the 1330s and continued at least until 1450 and possibly until the end of the fifteenth century. Their tiles were laid in Trinity Hospital, Leicester, sometime after 1331 and at Beauvale Priory in Nottinghamshire sometime

70 Three designs based on the arms of Ferrers used by the Nottingham tilers, later fourteenth century. The design showing the arms with a label of three points is the most accurate. The other two demonstrate the way in which the heraldry became debased when existing designs were copied inaccurately. 133–143 mm square.

after its foundation in 1343. Hugh le Tyler was working in Nottingham in 1377. Stephanus Tyler and Willelmus Grey 'Tyler' are known to have been working in Nottingham between 1480 and 1500, but it is more likely that at this time they were making roof tiles or even bricks as the word 'tile' was still sometimes, confusingly, used for bricks. There are, however, a number of fifteenth-century tiles known in Nottinghamshire and Leicestershire that could perhaps have been made in Nottingham itself.

The Nottingham tilers employed heraldry 70 extensively in their designs, which suggests that the originals were made for specific customers, but, as almost everywhere else, they continued to sell such tiles to anyone who wanted them. The decoration of their fifteenth-century tiles is inferior to that of their earlier products. It is not certain how tilers in the Midlands applied their white clay, but it forms a shallow layer in the cavities and may have been inserted as a thick slip.

GREAT MALVERN
During the 1450s the priory church at Great Malvern was rebuilt in fashionable perpendicular style and its floor paved with decorated two-colour tiles. These were made within the precinct, east of the church, where the remains of a kiln and a drying oven have been found. Great Malvern Priory was a cell of Westminster Abbey and it is possible that the tilers came from Westminster. The decoration of the tiles, however, was designed for the priory itself, including not only the Royal Arms and the 72 Arms of Westminster but also the arms of benefactors and crowned double M monograms for the dedication of the church to St Mary the Virgin and St Mary Magdalen.

Wherever they came from, the tilers were experts and reproduced these intricate heraldic designs and others including inscriptions with great accuracy. They stamped a shallow cavity in the surface of the tile and introduced white clay as a thin slip, probably pouring it through a perforated cow's horn. The slip clung to the edges of the cavity when it shrank, and this proved to be a very successful technique. Besides the usual paving tiles they also made

71 *Above* Design including the arms and name of Thomas Sebrok, Abbot of Gloucester, and the date 1455; from an early colour plate published by Henry Shaw in 1858. It was used by the Great Malvern tilers in the pavement of the Sanctuary in Gloucester Cathedral. Each tile 140 mm square.

72 *Right* Part of a panel of five wall tiles from Great Malvern Priory church. The decoration includes the Royal arms and sacred monogram within detailed architectural canopies. They were made by the Great Malvern tilers for the Priory church. The top tile of this panel, not illustrated here, includes the inscription 36 H V1, which was 1458/9, the latest date to be included in the Great Malvern designs. Each tile 220 × 160 mm.

wall tiles, many of which are still in position in the reredos behind the high altar in the priory church. These tiles are large and thick. For the first time, dates were included in the decoration: 1453, 1456 and 1458/9. During this period the Great Malvern tilers also made the tiles for Abbot Sebrok's pavement before the high altar in Gloucester Cathedral, where the designs include the abbot's name and arms and the date 1455. These men made their tiles of local Malvernian clay, which contains diagnostic features and is limited to a narrow band on the east side of the Malvern Hills. Because of this, their products can be recognised.

After they had finished their work at Great Malvern the tilers dispersed, taking some of their stamps with them. Their tiles have been found at various sites in the Severn Basin and up the Avon as far as Stratford and Warwick. One or more of them set up a kiln at Lenton Priory outside Nottingham, where its remains were excavated in 1955. The waste associated with this kiln consisted entirely of tiles decorated with Malvern designs. A few tiles decorated with Malvern designs had already been recognised in Nottingham and at least one tile had been found in York, but whether this came from the Lenton kiln or whether a tiler moved on as far as York is not known.

SIXTEENTH-CENTURY TILES

One or more of the Malvern tilers may have travelled south to Bristol and worked for St Augustine's Abbey, but no Malvern designs were used there and the work at Bristol was several decades later. The only real connection between the two centres is in the use of the poured slip technique. The tiles made for St Augustine's Abbey at the end of the fifteenth century and the beginning of the sixteenth were again designed to include heraldry and rebuses connected with the abbey, as well as inscriptions, but unfortunately no dates. The arms of John Newland and Robert Eliot place this work to the period between 1481 and 1515. The Bristol tilers were not using Malvernian clays, nor has the site of their tilery been located. The tiles in the pavement of Canynge's House in Bristol, now exhibited in the British Museum,

73 Another remarkable design with intricate, legible inscriptions including the date 1456, used by the Great Malvern tilers in the Priory church. 138 mm square.

are products of the Bristol tilers, all of them seconds as a result of opaque patches caused by tin in the glaze. The same tilers probably made the tiles designed for Edward Stafford, Duke of Buckingham, for use in Thornbury Castle. Stafford was executed in 1521, which provides a terminal date for this work, but the tilers sold the surplus tiles for use in other places.

Tilers using the poured slip technique travelled as far as Pembrokeshire, where tiles decorated with Bristol designs were laid in the cathedral at St David's, and new designs were made for Rhys ap Thomas, Lord of Carew, who died in 1525.

During the last decades before its dissolution in 1539, Hailes Abbey carried out some refurbishment which included repaving the chapter house and probably other parts of the buildings with a particularly beautiful series of tiles decorated in the same technique. Among the designs were the Royal Arms, the arms of Richard of Cornwall and the fleur-de-lis for the Virgin, to whom the church was dedicated, as well as monograms and rebuses of Thomas Stafford and Anthony Melton who ruled the house from 1483 to 1527. The designs also include a pomegranate, the badge of Catherine of Aragon, which would not have been made after 1533, when she was divorced.

74 *Opposite* Four tiles from Gloucester Cathedral. The decoration includes the rhebuses of John Nailheart and Robert Eliot on shields. Nailheart and Eliot were successively Abbots of St Augustine's, Bristol, from 1481 to 1515. The tiles were doubtless designed and made by expert tilers specially for St Augustine's Abbey church but they were also distributed in the surrounding area. Approx. 118 mm square.

75 One of the elaborate sixteen-tile designs included in the pavement of a chamber in Canynges House, Redcliffe Street, Bristol. See also Fig. 78.

76 A sixteen-tile design present on tiles from Hailes Abbey and Southam de la Bere, Gloucestershire. It includes the rhebus of Thomas Stafford, Abbot of Hailes from 1483 until succeeded by Anthony Melton before 1509, exact date unknown.

77 *Above* A design using the arms of Rhys ap Thomas, Lord of Carew, who died in 1525, present on the tiles in Carew Cheriton church, Dyfed. Probably made by tilers who moved from Bristol to St David's to pave the cathedral there.

78 *Right* A complete pavement from Canynges House, Redcliffe Street, Bristol, *c.*1480–1515. The decoration on some of the tiles includes the monogram of Robert Eliot on a shield (see also Fig. 74) and it can be assumed that the Canynges tiles were made by the same Bristol tilers as made those for St Augustine's Abbey. See also Fig. 75.

79 A sixteen-tile design present on tiles from Hailes Abbey, Gloucestershire. It includes the initials, name and rhebuses of Anthony Melton, Abbot of Hailes from before 1509 to 1527.

80 *Opposite* Tiles from Southam de la Bere, second quarter of the sixteenth century. Designed for Hailes Abbey, the tiles include the fleur-de-lis for the Virgin to whom the church was dedicated, the arms of Poitou for Richard of Cornwall the founder, and the monogram of Abbot Thomas Stafford. See also Fig. 76. 145–150 mm square.

This suggests that these pavements may have been laid before that date. The decoration is applied in poured slip and we may suppose that the tilers either came from Bristol or were successors of those who worked there for St Augustine's Abbey.

Other tilers were working in Dorset during the earlier sixteenth century. They seem to have applied their white clay as a shallow inlay rather than a poured slip. A comparable technique was used by tilers working on a series designed for William Sharington, the first lay owner of Lacock Abbey, between 1550, when he married his third wife, and 1553 when he died. These are the latest two-colour tiles to which a date can be given. Meanwhile, a fine series of designs were made for Fountains Abbey and other sites in

Yorkshire, and the tilers were almost certainly working in York itself. The tiles that they made were of a sound fabric but although they applied the decoration in poured slip, they had lost the art of doing this satisfactorily and the resulting decoration is erratic.

The main period of production of decorated medieval floor tiles lasted from the thirteenth to the mid-sixteenth century. During this period they achieved great popularity and provided vivid patterned pavements in royal palaces, ecclesiastical and monastic buildings and prosperous merchants' houses. Their rich, warm colours contrasted with the gilded mouldings and brilliant wall-paintings of the great Gothic buildings. The earliest pavements specially commissioned for wealthy patrons were decorated with beautiful and elaborate designs.

Commercial production began in the late decades of the thirteenth century, enabling any man who could afford a craftsman-built house to enjoy decorated tile pavements providing him with attractive, flat, hard-wearing floors. Inevitably the quality of design deteriorated during the fourteenth century until in the earlier fifteenth century it became very poor indeed.

A great revival began with the mid-fifteenth-century tilers who worked at Great Malvern Priory, setting up their tilery on the site in the old way and decorating their tiles with specially prepared and intricate designs. For the next hundred years wealthy patrons were ordering pavements designed for them, the decoration including their arms, badges, rebuses and initials. Commercial production continued in some areas and frequently the quality of decoration was unaffected by this revival as can be seen for example in the products of the Little Brickhill tilery.

The manufacture of hand-made roof tiles has continued until the present day as has that of both glazed and unglazed floor tiles although during the nineteenth and twentieth centuries most of these tiles have been made by machine. Few if any two-colour tiles are known to have been made after the 1550s. The quality of most of the sixteenth-century examples described above demonstrates that this industry did not

81 *Previous spread Left* Four tiles from Thornbury Castle decorated with the arms, supporters, Garter and badges of Edward Stafford, Duke of Buckingham. Designed before his execution in 1521 and probably made by the Bristol tilers.

82 *Previous spread Right* Part of a panel of tiles all from St George's Church, Fordington, Dorset, except that decorated with a heraldic shield. Those from Fordington were made there by local tilers during the first half of the sixteenth century.

83 *Right* Two tiles designed for William Sharrington, first lay owner of Lacock Abbey, Wiltshire, between 1550 and 1553. Possibly made by the same tilers as those from Fordington. See Fig. 79.

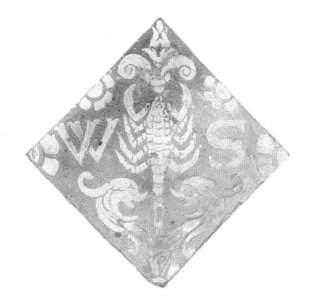

84 A four-tile design of the late fifteenth and early sixteenth century, which includes the arms of Fountains Abbey, Yorkshire, and the words BENEDICITE FONTES DOMINO, present on tiles from Fountains and Rievaulx Abbeys. Probably made by tilers working in York, where a contemporary tile kiln was found in the nineteenth century.

fail because of lack of expertise as has sometimes been suggested. The tiles were an integral part of the decoration of Gothic buildings and when Gothic architecture went out of fashion so did the two-colour tiles.

The revival of interest in Gothic architecture and the restoration of so many Gothic churches during the nineteenth century created a great demand for replicas of the medieval decorated tiles, particularly those with two-colour dec-oration, and from the 1830s onwards they were produced in increasing numbers. At first they were hand made using plastic clay but soon more intensive factory production was introduced mainly using pressed ceramic dust. The nineteenth-century manufacturers were proud to be able to produce flawless tiles all of the same even colour. These lack the individual variety of colour and texture of the medieval tilers' products, caused by impurities in the clay and glazes and the gases in the wood-fired kilns. Nevertheless the better nineteenth-century tiles were decorated with exact replicas of the medieval designs and in some places, such as Salisbury Chapter House, the Sanctuary of Great Malvern Priory church and the west end of Westminster Chapter House, the architects had an exact copy of the medieval arrangement of the pavement reproduced. In many places they saved the best preserved of the medieval tiles and we owe it to them and to other interested antiquarians that so many remain today.

PLACES TO VISIT

Select places where medieval tiles can be seen in their original position or re-set

Byland Abbey, Yorkshire: church, cloister and site museum
Canterbury Cathedral, Kent
Carew Cheriton Church, Dyfed
Chester Cathedral, Cheshire
Cleeve Abbey, Somerset: old refectory and church
Clifton House, King's Lynn, Norfolk
Ely Cathedral, Cambridgeshire
Ely, Cambridgeshire: Prior Crauden's chapel
Fountains Abbey, Yorkshire: church and site museum
Gloucester Cathedral, Gloucestershire
Great Linford Church, Buckinghamshire
Great Malvern Priory, Worcestershire
Higham Ferrers Church, Northamptonshire
Horwood Church, North Devon
Icklingham All Saints Church, Suffolk
Launcells Church, Cornwall
Milton Abbas, Dorset: St Catherine's chapel
Muchelney Church, Somerset
Newton St Petroc Church, North Devon
Old Byland Church, Yorkshire
Old Radnor Church, Powys
Rievaulx Abbey, Yorkshire: church, frater and site museum
Rochester Cathedral, Kent
St David's Cathedral, Dyfed
Shaftesbury Abbey, Dorset: church and site museum
Stokesay Castle, Shropshire
Stokesay Church, Shropshire
Strata Florida Abbey, Dyfed
Tewkesbury Abbey, Gloucestershire
Titchfield Abbey, Hampshire
Wells Cathedral, Somerset
West Leigh Church, North Devon
Westminster Abbey: Chapter House and St Faith's chapel
Winchester Cathedral, Hampshire
Winchester, Hampshire: Hospital of St Cross

Places with interesting replicas of medieval pavements

Great Malvern Priory, Worcestershire
Rochester Cathedral, Kent
St Alban's Abbey, Hertfordshire
Salisbury Cathedral Chapter House, Wiltshire
Winchester Cathedral, Hampshire

Select list of museums with displays of medieval tiles

British Museum, London
Bedford Museum, Bedfordshire
Birmingham City Museum and Art Gallery, West Midlands
Cheltenham Museum, Gloucestershire
Chertsey Museum, Surrey
Grosvenor Museum, Chester, Cheshire
Guildford Museum, Surrey
Hailes Abbey Site museum, Gloucestershire
Lacock Abbey, Wiltshire
Muchelney Abbey site museum, Somerset
Norton Priory Museum, Runcorn, Cheshire
St Ives Museum, Cambridgeshire
Salisbury Museum, Wiltshire
Thornton Abbey site museum, Humberside
Victoria and Albert Museum, London
Weybridge Museum, Surrey
Yorkshire Museum, York

Most county and town museums display some medieval tiles

FURTHER READING

The most extensive published bibliography and discussion of English medieval tiles are in the writer's catalogue of tiles in the British Museum listed below. A large number of articles are contained in national and local archaeological and antiquarian periodicals. A selection of the most useful books and papers is listed below.

General

ELIZABETH EAMES, *English Medieval Tiles*, British Museum Press, 1985.

ELIZABETH EAMES and THOMAS FANNING, *Irish Medieval Tiles*, Royal Irish Academy, Monographs in Archaeology 2, Royal Irish Academy, Dublin, 1988.

ANNE KELLOCK, 'Abbot Sebrok's pavement: a medieval tile floor in Gloucester Cathedral', *TBGAS*, 107 (1989).

JOHN GOUGH NICHOLS, *Examples of Decorative Tiles, sometimes termed encaustic*, London, 1845.

HENRY SHAW, *Specimens of Tile Pavements*, London, 1858.

J. B. WARD PERKINS, 'English Medieval Embossed tiles', *Archaeological Journal*, Vol. XCIV, 1937.

Catalogues

ELIZABETH EAMES, *Catalogue of Medieval Lead-glazed Earthernware Tiles in the Department of Medieval and Later Antiquities, British Museum*, London, 1980.

ELIZABETH EAMES, 'Tiles' in Peter and Eleanor Saunders *Salisbury and South Wiltshire Museum Medieval Catalogue*, Part I, 1991.

ARTHUR LANE, *A Guide to the Collection of Tiles*, Victoria and Albert Museum, London, 1939, 2nd edn, 1960, chs III and IV.

J. B. WARD PERKINS, *London Museum Catalogues, No.7 Medieval Catalogue*, London, 1940.

Regional

PHILIP B. CHATWIN, 'The Medieval Patterned Tiles of Warwickshire', *Transactions of the Birmingham . . . Archaeological Society*, Vol. LX (1936), pub. 1940.

ELIZABETH EAMES, 'The Products of a Medieval Tile Kiln at Bawsey, King's Lynn', *Antiquaries Journal*, Vol. XXXV, 1955.
    'The Canynges Pavement', *Journal of the British Archaeological Association*, Vol. XIV, 1951.
    'A Tile Pavement from the Queen's Chamber, Clarendon Palace, dated 1250–2' ibid., Vols XX, XXI, 1957–8.
    'A Thirteenth-century tile pavement from the King's Chapel, Clarendon Palace', ibid., Vol. XXVI, 1963.

ELIZABETH EAMES and LAURENCE KEEN, 'Some line-impressed mosaic from western England and Wales', *Journal of the British Archaeological Association*, Vol. XXXV, 1972.

A. B. EMDEN, *Medieval Decorated Tiles in Dorset*, Chichester, 1977.

B. W. GREENFIELD, 'Encaustic Tiles of the Middle Ages . . . in the South of Hampshire', *Proceedings of the Hampshire Field Club*, Vol. II, Part II, 1892.

LOYD HABERLY, *Medieval English Pavingtiles*, Oxford, 1937.

CHRISTOPHER HOHLER, 'Medieval Pavingtiles in Buckinghamshire', *Records of Buckinghamshire*, Vol. XIV, 1942.

LAURENCE KEEN, 'A Series of 17th- and 18th-century lead-glazed relief tiles from North Devon', *Journal of the British Archaeological Association*, Vol. XXXII, 1969.

G. E. C. KNAPP, 'The Medieval Paving Tiles of the Alton area of N.E. Hampshire', *Proceedings of the Hampshire Field Club and Archaeological Society*, Vol. XVIII, 1954.

J. M. LEWIS, *Welsh Medieval Paving Tiles*, Department of Archaeology, National Museum of Wales, 1976.

MANWARING SHURLOCK, *Tiles from Chertsey Abbey, Surrey, representing early romance subjects*, London, 1885.

NORMA WHITCOMB, *The Medieval Floor-Tiles of Leicestershire*, Leicester, 1956.

Kilns

PAUL J. DRURY and G. D. PRATT, 'A late 13th- and early 14th-century tile factory at Danbury, Essex', *Medieval Archaeology*, Vol. 19, 1975.

ELIZABETH EAMES, 'A Thirteenth-century Tile Kiln Site at North Grange, Meaux, Beverley, Yorkshire', *Medieval Archaeology*, Vol. V, 1961.

J. S. GARDNER and ELIZABETH EAMES, 'A Tile Kiln at Chertsey Abbey', *Journal of the British Archaeological Association*, Vol. XVII, 1954.

T. B. JAMES and A. M. ROBINSON with ELIZABETH EAMES, *Clarendon Palace*, Antiquaries Research Report XLV, 1988 Part III, 'The tile kiln and floor tiles'.

DENNIS C. MYNARD, 'The Little Brickhill tile kilns and their products', *Journal of the British Archaeological Association*, Vol. 38, 1975.

J. S. RICHARDSON, 'A Thirteenth-century Tile Kiln at North Berwick, East Lothian . . .', *Proceedings of the Society of Antiquaries of Scotland*, Vol. LXIII, 1928–9.

LEOPOLD A. VIDLER, 'Floor Tiles and Kilns near the site of St Bartholomew's Hospital, Rye', *Sussex Archaeological Collections*, Vol. LXXIII, 1932.

ACKNOWLEDGEMENTS

The author's thanks are due to Celia Clear and Rachel Rogers of British Museum Press and to colleagues in the Department of Medieval and Later Antiquities in the British Museum and to Alison Mulcahy-Morgan for their help in the preparation of this book.

PHOTOGRAPHIC CREDITS

Amberley Chalk Pits Museum, Arundel. Photo: John Land: 8, 9; David Bacon: 66; John Bailey: 1, 68; James Barfoot: 28, 35, 36, 37, 38, 54, 64, 71; Kenneth Beaulah: 32; British Library, London: *front cover* (MS Harleian 2278, f.23), *title page* (Add MS 38122, f.78v), 4 (MS Stowe 594, f.5b); Trustees of the British Museum, London: 3, 10 (Drawn by Jim Farrant after Kenneth Beaulah), 11, 16, 17, 18, 19, 20, 21, 22, 23, 24, 25, 29, 30, 33, 39, 40, 43, 44, 48, 49, 50, 51, 52, 53, 55, 56, 57, 58, 62, 63, 67, 69, 70, 72, 73, 74, 75, 76, 77, 79, 80, 81, 82, 83, 84; John Charlton: 12; L.S. Colchester: 60; Paul Drury: 7; © Dulwich Picture Gallery, 1981: *contents page*; Elizabeth Eames: 6, 13, 14, 15, 21, 26, 34 (photo: James Barfoot, drawn by Rosemonde Nairac): 41, 42, 45 (drawn by Rosemonde Nairac): 46 (drawn by Rosemonde Nairac): 59, 61, 65, 78; Thomas Fanning: 27; © Farnham and District Museum Society, Nicholas Riall and Valerie Shelton-Bunn 1989. Drawn by Jim Farrant after Nicholas Riall: 5; Royal Commission for the Historical Monuments of England, London: 31, 47.